LONDON, NEW YORK,
MELBOURNE, MUNICH, AND DELHI

Senior Editor Alastair Dougall
Design Manager Robert Perry
Designers Nick Avery, Owen Bennett, Jon Hall,
Guy Harvey, Nathan Martin
Publishing Manager Simon Beecroft
Category Publisher Alex Allan
Production Controller Amy Bennett
Production Editor Siu Yin Chan

First published in Great Britain in 2009
by Dorling Kindersley Limited
80 Strand
London WC2R 0RL
A Penguin Company

2 4 6 8 10 9 7 5 3 1
WD210—01/09

A CIP record for this book is available from the British Library.

ISBN: 978-1-40533-895-0

Colour reproduction by Alta Image, UK
Printed and bound in China by Hung Hing Printing

Discover more at
www.dk.com

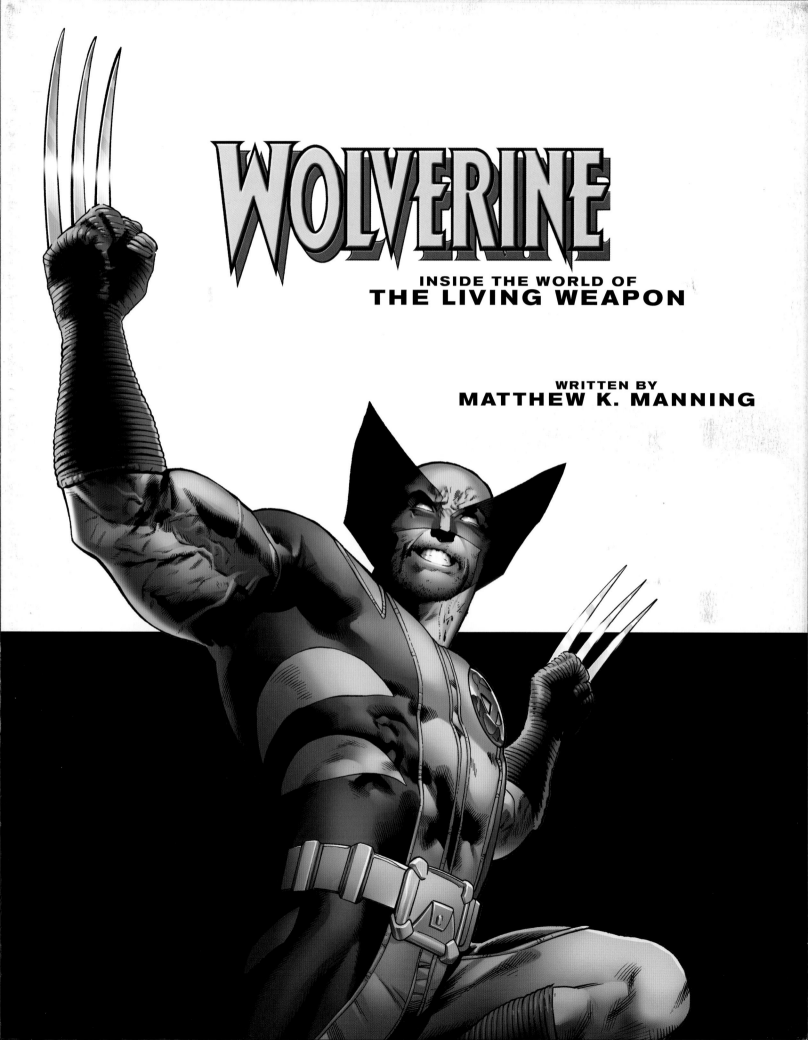

WOLVERINE

INSIDE THE WORLD OF
THE LIVING WEAPON

WRITTEN BY
MATTHEW K. MANNING

Contents

Wolverine. James Howlett. Logan. Skunk-Bear. Runt. Weapon X. Death. The ol' Canucklehead. He goes by many names, but no matter his moniker, one thing remains a constant: Wolverine is the best there is at what he does.

"I'M THE BEST THERE IS AT WHAT I DO BUT WHAT I DO BEST ISN'T VERY NICE."

FOREWORD

Seventeen (17) words—doesn't seem like much in the overall scheme of things, yet in the case of Wolverine, they represent the essence of my vision of his character. He's come a long way in the 30-plus years since Len Wein created him; he's changed a tremendous amount from that original conception—Dave Cockrum and I made him older, we made the adamantium claws a part of him, Dave created his distinctive facial features and hair; John Byrne and I broadened the way he functioned within the X-Men, as he gradually (but somehow inevitably) moved more and more center stage; Frank Miller and I took those initial character elements and both broadened and deepened them, fulfilling our ambition to make him an increasingly three-dimensional and real character. This is the Wolverine—the "Logan"—I choose to remember.

To me, he exemplifies the conflict faced by all the X-Men—only in his case, it's taken to perhaps its ultimate extreme. He faces the age-old conflict between good and evil—but it isn't an external challenge, it's internal, it's a struggle to define his very being as a man, as (perhaps) a hero. The struggle for him is both to define the goals of his life and then see if there are ways to achieve them. The ongoing temptation for him is whether or not to yield to what many refer to as the "animal" side of his nature, to follow in the footsteps of Sabretooth. There is a part of him that would very much like to yield to this siren-song, but it's countered by another part of him that's just as impassioned in its quest to embrace his humanity, who wants to live out his life to its fullest as a man. It's not the easiest of challenges but it's one that has defined the essence of this man for decades, and made him one of the most interesting characters (to write as much as to read) in the X-Men, if not in publishing.

I hope you enjoy this book as much as I've enjoyed telling these stories of his life.

CHRIS CLAREMONT

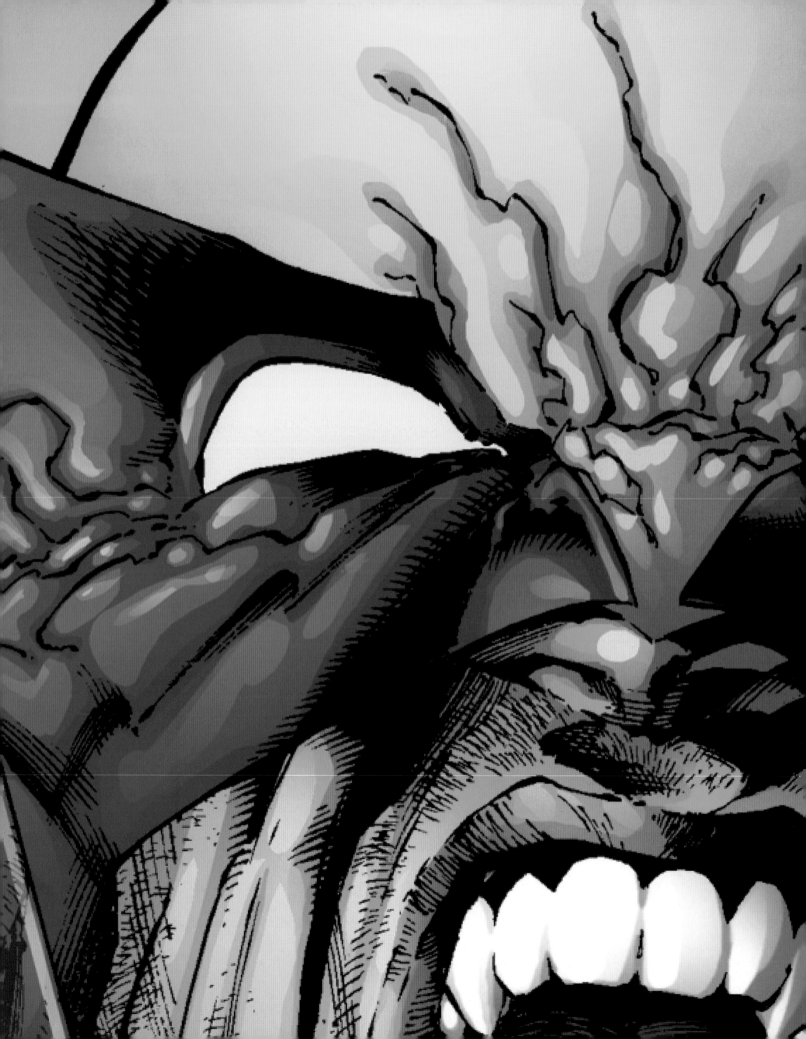

CHAPTER **ONE**

The Character of Wolverine

...FIVE THINGS YOU SHOULD KNOW ABOUT WOLVERINE...

1 Wolverine's real name is James Howlett, *NOT* Logan, which was an alias he adopted after fleeing his family home. Thomas Logan was the groundskeeper on the Howlett estate in Alberta, Canada.

2 Wolverine is over 100 years old, but his remarkable regenerative powers keep him looking as he did in his early forties.

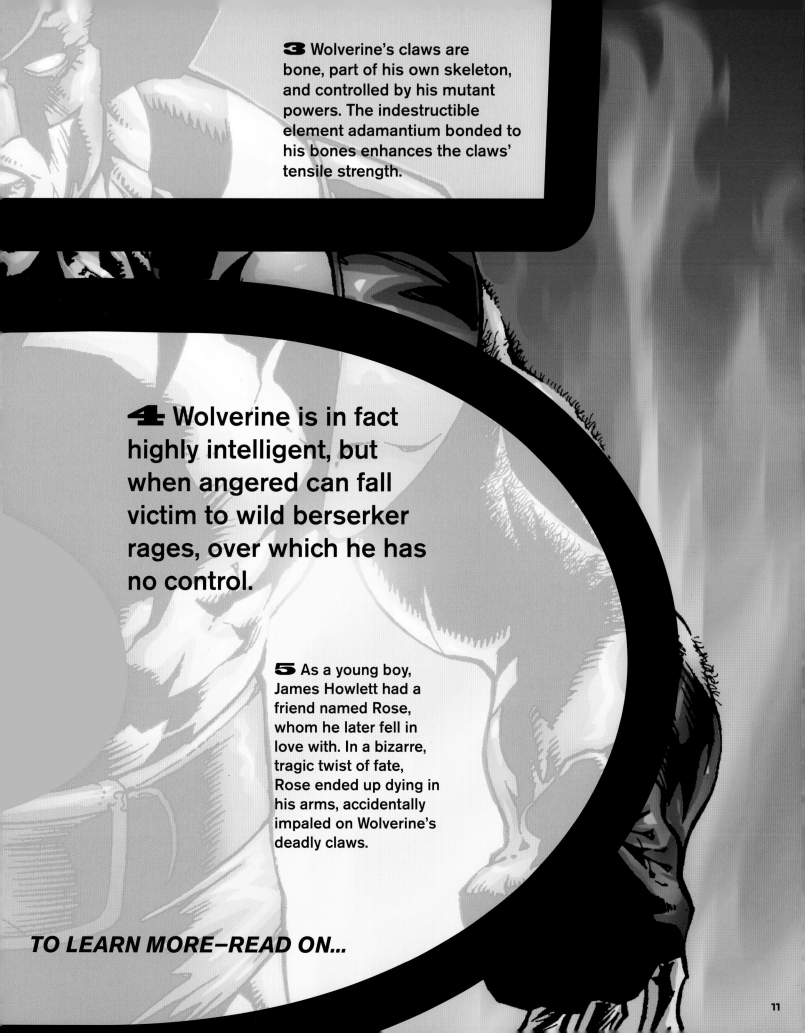

3 Wolverine's claws are bone, part of his own skeleton, and controlled by his mutant powers. The indestructible element adamantium bonded to his bones enhances the claws' tensile strength.

4 Wolverine is in fact highly intelligent, but when angered can fall victim to wild berserker rages, over which he has no control.

5 As a young boy, James Howlett had a friend named Rose, whom he later fell in love with. In a bizarre, tragic twist of fate, Rose ended up dying in his arms, accidentally impaled on Wolverine's deadly claws.

TO LEARN MORE—READ ON...

"IF YOU REALLY WANT TO TANGLE WITH SOMEONE...

...TRY YOUR LUCK AGAINST...

...the Wolverine!"

Wolverine can take a bullet. With his high tolerance to pain and mutant healing ability, he has proven that he can shrug off more than his fair share of spent ammunition. However, when the character was first being developed by writer Len Wein and artist John Romita Sr., it seemed that *dodging* bullets might be his greatest strength.

The first bullet was his name. Editor-in-Chief Roy Thomas decided that the Marvel Universe needed a character whose roots were planted firmly in the Canadian wilderness. Thomas toyed with the name Badger, before opting for Wolverine, an idea he passed to Wein to develop.

As Wein collaborated with art director, John Romita Sr., the character of Wolverine would dodge his second bullet. Knowing next to nothing about the animal in question, Romita was under the impression that a wolverine was a female wolf. Fortunately, this misconception was quickly discovered when Romita began to research the furry creature.

The final bullet Wolverine successfully dodged during his creation was his intended origin. Originally, Wein conceived Wolverine as simply a highly evolved version of his animal namesake. However, the notion of a talking woodland creature was soon nixed and the character given a more realistic background.

Wolverine's claws were always intended to be retractable; however Len Wein never intended for them to be a part of his actual body. Instead, Wein saw the claws as part of Wolverine's gloves, but was overruled by writer Chris Claremont, when Wolverine made his way onto the X-Men. Claremont thought that natural claws made the character irreplaceable.

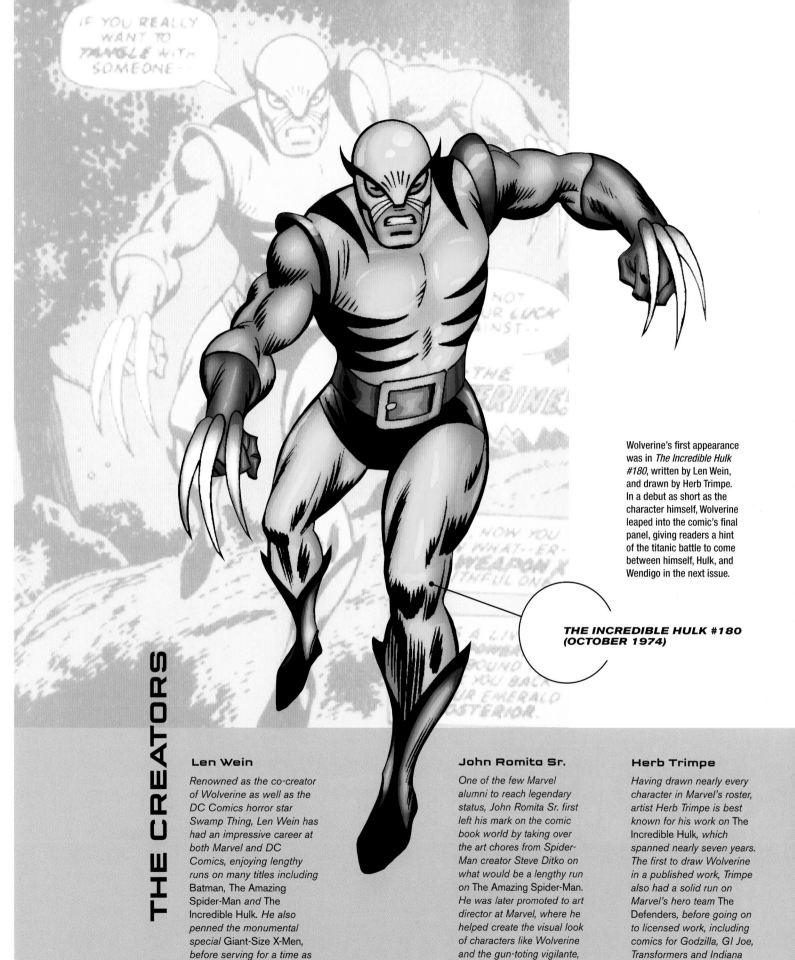

Wolverine's first appearance was in *The Incredible Hulk #180*, written by Len Wein, and drawn by Herb Trimpe. In a debut as short as the character himself, Wolverine leaped into the comic's final panel, giving readers a hint of the titanic battle to come between himself, Hulk, and Wendigo in the next issue.

THE INCREDIBLE HULK #180 (OCTOBER 1974)

THE CREATORS

Len Wein

Renowned as the co-creator of Wolverine as well as the DC Comics horror star Swamp Thing, Len Wein has had an impressive career at both Marvel and DC Comics, enjoying lengthy runs on many titles including Batman, The Amazing Spider-Man *and The Incredible Hulk. He also penned the monumental special* Giant-Size X-Men, *before serving for a time as Marvel's Editor-in-Chief.*

John Romita Sr.

One of the few Marvel alumni to reach legendary status, John Romita Sr. first left his mark on the comic book world by taking over the art chores from Spider-Man creator Steve Ditko on what would be a lengthy run on The Amazing Spider-Man. *He was later promoted to art director at Marvel, where he helped create the visual look of characters like Wolverine and the gun-toting vigilante, the Punisher.*

Herb Trimpe

Having drawn nearly every character in Marvel's roster, artist Herb Trimpe is best known for his work on The Incredible Hulk, *which spanned nearly seven years. The first to draw Wolverine in a published work, Trimpe also had a solid run on Marvel's hero team* The Defenders, *before going on to licensed work, including comics for Godzilla, GI Joe, Transformers and Indiana Jones.*

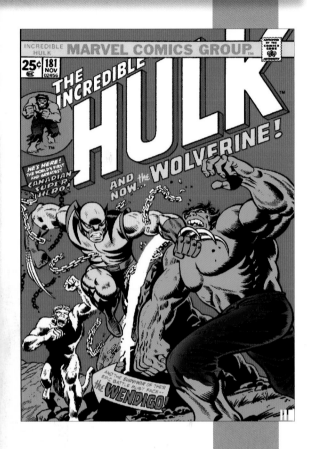

Publication date
November 1974

Editor-in-chief
Roy Thomas

Cover artist
Herb Trimpe

Writer
Len Wein

Penciller
Herb Trimpe

Inker
Jack Abel

Colorist
Glynis Wein

Letterer
Artie Simek

The Incredible HULK #181

> "**Little man tried to trick Hulk...
> but Hulk was smarter...
> Hulk was stronger...
> ... and that is why Hulk won!**"

HULK TO A DEFEATED WOLVERINE

MAIN CHARACTERS: Hulk, Wolverine, Wendigo
SUPPORTING CHARACTERS: George Baptiste, Holeridge,
Marie Cartier, Matthews
LOCATIONS: Quebec, Canada (including Department H)

Background

Roy Thomas had recently discovered Canada. In 1974, as editor-in-chief of Marvel Comics, Thomas had become aware that his company had been selling more and more comics to his country's northern neighbors, and therefore thought the creation of a Canadian Super Hero was in order. Inspired by the real-life woodland animal that finds its home on both sides of the American/Canadian border, Thomas handed over the character concept of Wolverine to *Incredible Hulk* scribe Len Wein with instructions to use this new creation in Hulk's own title. Wein shaped the hero into a "small, nasty guy," and passed the idea along to the art director, legendary Marvel artist John Romita Sr. Even though Wein had pictured Wolverine as a fiery teenage brawler, Romita gave the hero an older look. He researched the real-life wolverine animal and gave the character a height of just 5 ft 3 in to reflect the relatively small size of this fierce creature. And soon, with a one-panel introduction on the last page of issue *#180* of *The Incredible Hulk*, Wolverine was born, leaping into battle with a furious energy that would prove typical of the future hero's hair-trigger temper.

The Story

Wolverine makes his action-packed debut as he throws himself in between two seeming forces of nature, the incredible Hulk and the brutal woods-beast Wendigo...

Nothing in the life of Dr. Robert Bruce Banner ever went smoothly. First there were the gamma rays, the ones that transformed him from a simple mild mannered scientist into a raving behemoth known as the Hulk. Then there was the government. They'd pursued him in both of his identities, demanding Bruce Banner pay for the damage caused by his monstrous alter ego. Even when Banner tried to do good, things seemed to blow up in his extremely frightening face. Take his latest attempt at heroics. The Hulk traveled to Quebec, Canada at the insistence of the beautiful Marie Cartier in order to find a cure for the mythic albino monster, known only as the Wendigo, that haunted the nearby wilderness. But instead of helping the brutal beast the Hulk found himself battling him, the two nearly evenly matched in both strength and stamina. And if that wasn't bad enough, soon a third equally savage player entered the arena. A mean little man calling himself Wolverine.

Clad in a bright yellow uniform complete with drawn on whiskers and claws, Wolverine immediately leapt into the fray. A secret agent for Department H, a faction of the Canadian government, Wolverine, also known as Weapon X, was embarking on one of his first missions: to take down the Hulk using whatever means necessary. It was a formidable task, but one Wolverine didn't balk at, despite the noticeable size differential.

Using his speed to his advantage, Wolverine vaulted from the Hulk to the Wendigo, and back again, barely even coming into contact with the ground below. As ferocious as his namesake, Wolverine soon fell into favor with the Hulk, and teamed up with the Green Goliath in order to knock the Wendigo unconscious **(1)**. As the two took in a moment of silence to gaze at their fallen opponent, Wolverine quickly turned on the Hulk, taking the opportunity to catch his true target off guard.

While in a not-too-distant secret complex, military personnel argued over his capabilities **(2)**, Wolverine continued to battle the Hulk as night slowly gave way to the rising sun. Meanwhile, Marie Cartier along with her friend, Georges Baptiste, emerged from the nearby bushes and dragged Wendigo's limp body away from the conflict. As it turned out, Marie's brother was actually the Wendigo, the victim of an ancient curse that she intended to transfer to the Hulk through the use of the black arts. Though Georges seemed weary of Marie's plan, he nevertheless followed her as she cast the spell of subjugation **(3)**, creating an almost invisible gas that rendered both Wolverine and the Hulk unconscious **(4)**, and made the Hulk revert back to his form as Bruce Banner. Seeing Banner in his true form, Georges refused to be a part of Marie's twisted plan any longer, and left her to bind Wolverine by herself **(5)** in order to remove the mutant from the action. While she was otherwise occupied, Banner awoke from his slumber and changed back into the Hulk, now furious at Marie as well as Wolverine. As Marie ducked into a nearby cave, the Hulk shattered Wolverine's chains **(6)** so as to resume their fight unencumbered.

But their battle would be interrupted once more as Marie ran into the Wendigo itself in her attempt to flee, the young woman letting out a shrill scream that distracted Wolverine. The Hulk capitalized on his foe's momentary lapse, knocking the hero unconscious **(7)**, and then watched the Wendigo flee the nearby cave, followed by a distraught Marie Cartier. It seems that Marie's plot had worked indeed, but just not in the way she had devised. Yes, her brother was free of the Wendigo's curse, but at a high cost, as the creature's monstrous burden had been unwittingly transferred to her good friend, Georges Baptiste.

1

2

3

4

5

5

5

"Hulk will break little man's chains... and little man with them!"

6

Dressed TO KILL

Although he's comfortable fighting a barroom brawl in a leather jacket and jeans, Wolverine nevertheless feels the need to dress for the occasion, finding a proper uniform helps him to get in the right mindset to do what he does best.

1 X-MEN

The costume Logan wears most frequently is a variation on his original Wolverine uniform. While serving with the X-Men or off on his own adventures, Wolvie's classic blue and yellow duds let his opponents know exactly what kind of trouble is headed their way.

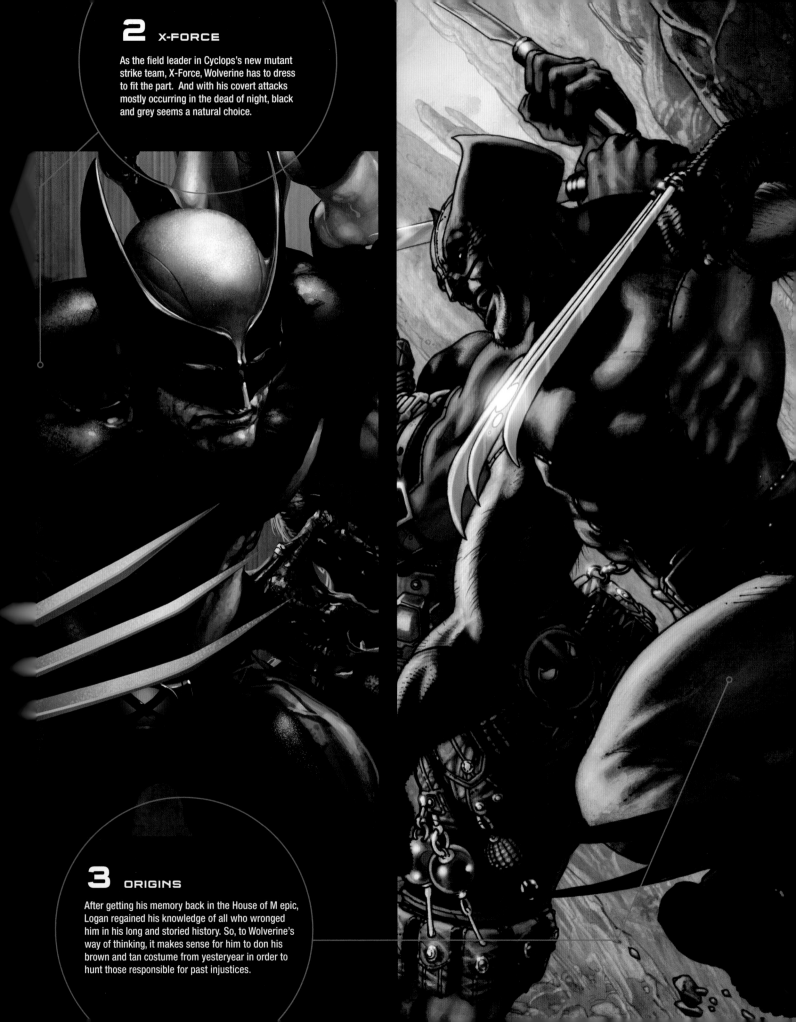

2 X-FORCE

As the field leader in Cyclops's new mutant strike team, X-Force, Wolverine has to dress to fit the part. And with his covert attacks mostly occurring in the dead of night, black and grey seems a natural choice.

3 ORIGINS

After getting his memory back in the House of M epic, Logan regained his knowledge of all who wronged him in his long and storied history. So, to Wolverine's way of thinking, it makes sense for him to don his brown and tan costume from yesteryear in order to hunt those responsible for past injustices.

WOLVERINE style

Over the years, Wolverine has undergone many a costume change, his look often representing a new era or incarnation of his team, the X-Men. But when not dressed in full battle gear, Logan's unique style proclaims his outsider stance.

As co-owner of the Princess Bar, a small saloon in the island nation of Madripoor, Wolverine sometimes feels the need to dress up. Perhaps in an attempt to give his establishment the same air as a classic film from cinema's golden age.

Wolverine can often be seen grabbing a beer at a local pub and wearing nothing more than a dirty undershirt and jeans. Logan knows from experience that nice clothes only get ruined in the likely event of a bar fight breaking out.

Even though Logan spent months nude in the freezing wilds of Canada in his past, these days he'd much rather throw on a coat and boots when heading to colder climates.

Whether tracking an adversary or just minding his own business, there are two items of clothing Wolverine favors. The first is a leather jacket, giving him a mean and moody, "Rebel Without a Cause" look—though Wolverine has plenty of reasons to rebel. The second is a cowboy hat he acquired in a fight with Sabretooth many years ago.

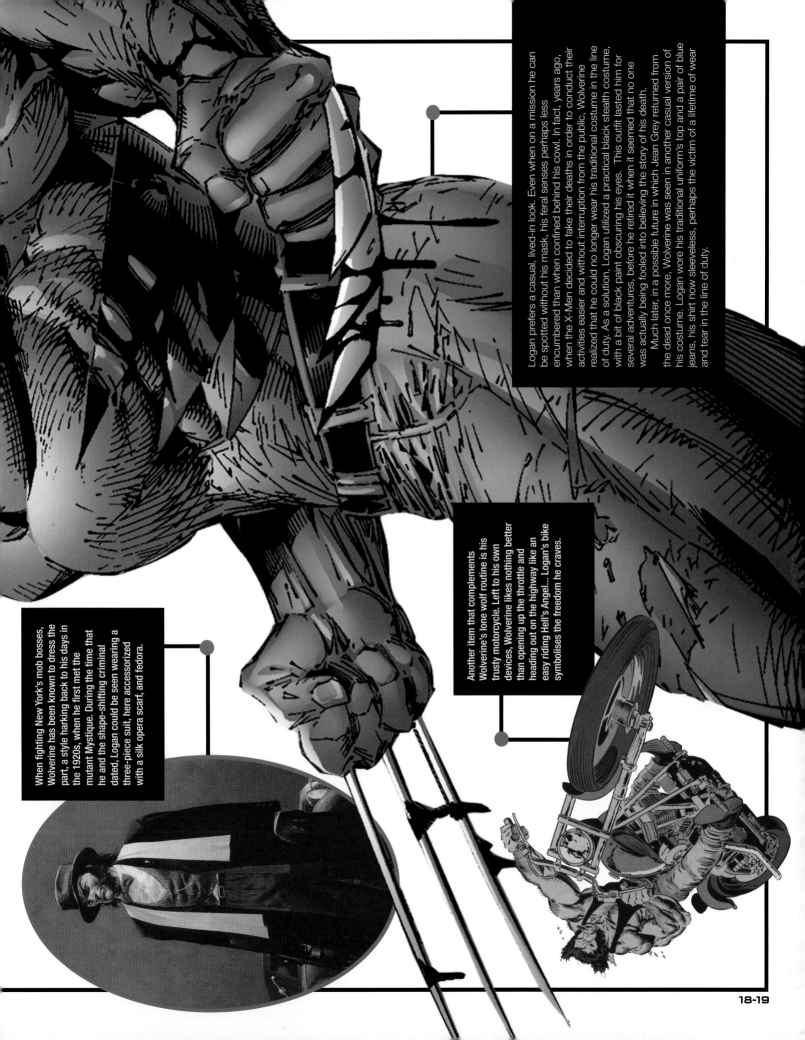

Logan prefers a casual, lived-in look. Even when on a mission he can be spotted without his mask, his feral senses perhaps less encumbered than when confined behind his cowl. In fact, years ago, when the X-Men decided to fake their deaths in order to conduct their activities easier and without interruption from the public, Wolverine realized that he could no longer wear his traditional costume in the line of duty. As a solution, Logan utilized a practical black stealth costume, with a bit of black paint obscuring his eyes. This outfit lasted him for several adventures, before he retired it when it seemed that no one was actually being fooled into believing the story of his death.

Much later, in a possible future in which Jean Grey returned from the dead once more, Wolverine was seen in another casual version of his costume. Logan wore his traditional uniform's top and a pair of blue jeans, his shirt now sleeveless, perhaps the victim of a lifetime of wear and tear in the line of duty.

Another item that complements Wolverine's lone wolf routine is his trusty motorcycle. Left to his own devices, Wolverine likes nothing better than opening up the throttle and heading out on the highway like an easy riding Hell's Angel... Logan's bike symbolises the freedom he craves.

When fighting New York's mob bosses, Wolverine has been known to dress the part, a style harking back to his days in the 1920s, when he first met the mutant Mystique. During the time that he and the shape-shifting criminal dated, Logan could be seen wearing a three-piece suit, here accessorized with a silk opera scarf, and fedora.

POWERS

ALTHOUGH WOLVERINE IS NOT DEFINED SOLELY BY HIS SUPERHUMAN ABILITIES, THEY DO COME IN HANDY IN A FIGHT

When his mutant powers were activated, James Howlett went from being a weak and sickly adolescent to a life as a clawed, super-strong fighting machine. His dormant abilities were triggered by the stress of seeing his father murdered before his eyes. That traumatic moment forever shattered James's seemingly normal life.

HEALING FACTOR

Probably the biggest advantage garnered by Wolverine's mutant genetic makeup is his uncanny ability to heal rapidly from virtually any wound inflicted upon him. This healing process is many times quicker than the average man's, but varies in speed depending on the severity of the wound. During his adventures, Wolverine has bounced back from having his body shot, burned, and stabbed. His mutant abilities also enable him to heal rapidly from poisons and disease, and resist the ravages of old age. Despite being more than a hundred years old, Logan only appears to be in his early forties because of his amazing mutant healing factor.

FERAL SENSES

Due to his mutant gene, Wolverine possesses incredibly fine-tuned senses. He can see in near pitch darkness, and view an enemy perfectly from far distances. His sense of smell rivals that of the finest hunting dog, and allows him to track a target for miles. His hearing is so acute, he can identify an unseen threat from blocks away, just by detecting the slightest rustling of clothing.

ADAMANTIUM

When captured by the clandestine Weapon X program, Wolverine's bones were bonded with adamantium, a virtually unbreakable metal. The weight of metal in his body increases Logan's strength and density, and helps protect his vital inner organs.

PHYSICAL STRENGTH

Wolverine's already extraordinary strength is increased by his adamantium-enhanced skeleton. Possessing punches that feel like a collision with solid steel, Wolverine can lift between 600 and 800 lbs (272 and 363 kg). He also possesses superhuman endurance, speed, and stamina, and when in one of his mindless berserker rages he is capable of releasing a barrage of attacks in a few frenzied moments.

THE CLAWS

Wolverine's claws first sprang from his fists after a traumatic encounter triggered his latent mutant abilities when he was a young boy. First consisting only of rock-hard bone, his claws were later laced with adamantium, making them unbreakable and able to cut through nearly any known surface. Wolverine maintains absolute control over his claws, and can "pop" one at a time if it suits his purposes. The skin on his hands breaks each time the claws emerge.

Fightin' MAD!

With his unique combination of brute strength and training, Wolverine is the perfect fighting machine.

He punches with the power of a freight train. His body is always at the peak of human perfection. And he has a near limitless internal catalog of learned martial arts techniques to pick and choose from. Even without his enhanced senses and razor-sharp claws, Wolverine can best most any opponent foolish enough to face him. But when combined with his feral nature, instinctive predatory abilities, healing factor, and adamantium-laced bones, Wolverine is an almost unstoppable threat.

In an attempt to keep his berserker animalistic nature in check, Wolverine has traveled all over the globe mastering civilized fighting styles. Besides the training he underwent in order to become a member of the CIA and Canadian military, Wolverine has studied under a variety of masters in a variety of countries. In Japan, he studied under Ogun, a master who had no peer in his day. Wolverine also journeyed to Jasmine Falls in order to study under Bando Suboro, and later had his anger forged into a tangible weapon by the fabled immortal known as Muramasa.

Through the years, with the help of other instructors, Wolverine built upon the techniques he acquired from these masters. He perfected his fighting styles training with the mercenary Cyber and in various military institutions. With this vast bank of martial arts knowledge to draw from, combined with his considerable experience in battle and his training beside Professor Charles Xavier and his mutant teammates in the X-Men, Wolverine is a master of virtually every fighting style known to man or mutant.

SUPERHUMAN STRENGTH

Besides being a natural born brawler, Wolverine was also blessed with a degree of superhuman strength alongside his other mutant abilities. When his skeleton was bonded with unbreakable adamantium by the clandestine Weapon X project, his inherent power was increased as well, with reinforced bones that added about 100 lbs to his already hefty small frame. Wolverine's powerful blows are capable of giving even Marvel's mightiest heavyweights, such as the Incredible Hulk and Colossus, a moment's pause.

A GIGANTIC SENTINEL ROBOT PROVES NO MATCH FOR WOLVERINE

Always on top!

5 OF WOLVERINE'S UNBELIEVABLE BATTLES

1 Despite being unable to breath underwater, Wolverine once faced down the aquatic villain Tiger Shark, and narrowly avoided drowning when his claws became embedded in a coral reef. He later bested the villain in a fierce battle in a helicopter, knocking Tiger Shark into the water below and into the jaws of the villain's hungry namesake.

2 While in China, Wolverine found himself locked in combat with the mysterious White Shadow and Black Shadow, seemingly indestructible energy creatures. Tracking the mystical enigmas back to their lair, Wolverine was finally able to defeat these untouchable manifestations by destroying their host body.

3 On a mission to destroy the high priest of the secret criminal organization called the Hand, Logan fought his way through hundreds upon hundreds of expert ninjas in search of the villain known as Gorgon. He also had help help from his old friend and brilliant martial artist in her own right, Elektra.

4 While being pursued by a near-unbeatable combination of mind-controlled versions of his former X-Men allies, Phoenix, Rogue and Psylocke, as well as martial artists Jessica Drew, Yukio, and Tyger Tiger, Wolverine defeated his brainwashed friends and his own feral rage with the help of former sidekicks Jubilee and Shadowcat.

5 In Belgium during World War I, as he fought for the Canadian cause, Wolverine encountered Lazaer, also known as Azrael, the angel of death himself. Undaunted by his supernatural opponent, Logan seemingly killed his foe by impaling him through the chest with his own sword.

It's probably his most powerful weapon. Wolverine was born a mutant, possessing an enhanced X gene in his genetic makeup. Like most of his kind, his abilities were triggered during his adolescence. From that time forward, Logan has found his body has the amazing ability to recover from most any wound. When combined with his unbreakable adamantium skeleton, he becomes almost indestructible, and has proven over the years that he's able to bounce back from any injury, given time for his body to knit itself back together.

Wolverine's body is able to grow back damaged tissue, fight off disease and infection at a rapid rate, retard the normal human aging process, and quickly battle most poisons and drugs. It has also been theorized that some of Wolverine's most traumatic memories have been eradicated by this same mutant ability, in an attempt by his body to protect his mental health.

During the **Civil War**, Wolverine was turned into a fireball by Nitro, but he emerged with only slightly singed hair.

The HEALING FACTOR

Both Wolverine and Sabretooth possess the uncanny mutant power to heal both muscle and skin tissue, an ability that only serves to prolongs their violent clashes.

10 things Wolverine has survived

"I got no problem with pain. Me and pain are old friends."

1 Logan proved just how bulletproof he was when he received a gunshot in the forehead while facing off against a Japanese crime family.

2 Fighting alongside the Silver Samurai, Wolverine once had the majority of his skin burnt in an explosion and his adamantium skull partially exposed.

3 Wolverine's body was sent into shock when Magneto ripped out the adamantium metal coating his skeleton. Logan just barely pullied through the trauma.

4 When fighting the anti-hero the Punisher, Wolverine was run over by a steamroller but still managed to survive.

5 While partnering with Daredevil and Spider-Man, Logan was shot by a bazooka, but lived to fight again.

6 After escaping a Japanese prison camp near the end of World War II, Wolverine recovered despite being trapped in the nuclear blast at Hiroshima.

7 Logan was left for dead after being blown up by a bomb by an agent of the terrorist organization known as Scimitar.

8 Wolverine once deliberately set off an explosion in a car he was in so, as a supposed corpse, he would be carried behind enemy lines unnoticed.

9 Trapped on an asteroid headed for the sun, Logan opened a hatch and exposed himself to the star. Badly burned, he was saved by Phoenix.

10 Caught in an artificial nuclear explosion caused by the villain Nitro, Wolverine's adamantium-enhanced skeleton was forced to heal itself from scratch.

The New Deal

But there are some injuries even a mutant healing factor can't mend. When Wolverine pushes himself past the limits of his regenerative abilities, he finds himself in a limbo of sorts, facing off against Lazaer, the angel of death. Only by winning these duels can Logan continue to return to the land of the living. Recently Wolverine struck up a bargain with Lazaer in order to regain a piece of his soul. In exchange, not only is Logan's healing factor less powerful, but now he can no longer return from the dead.

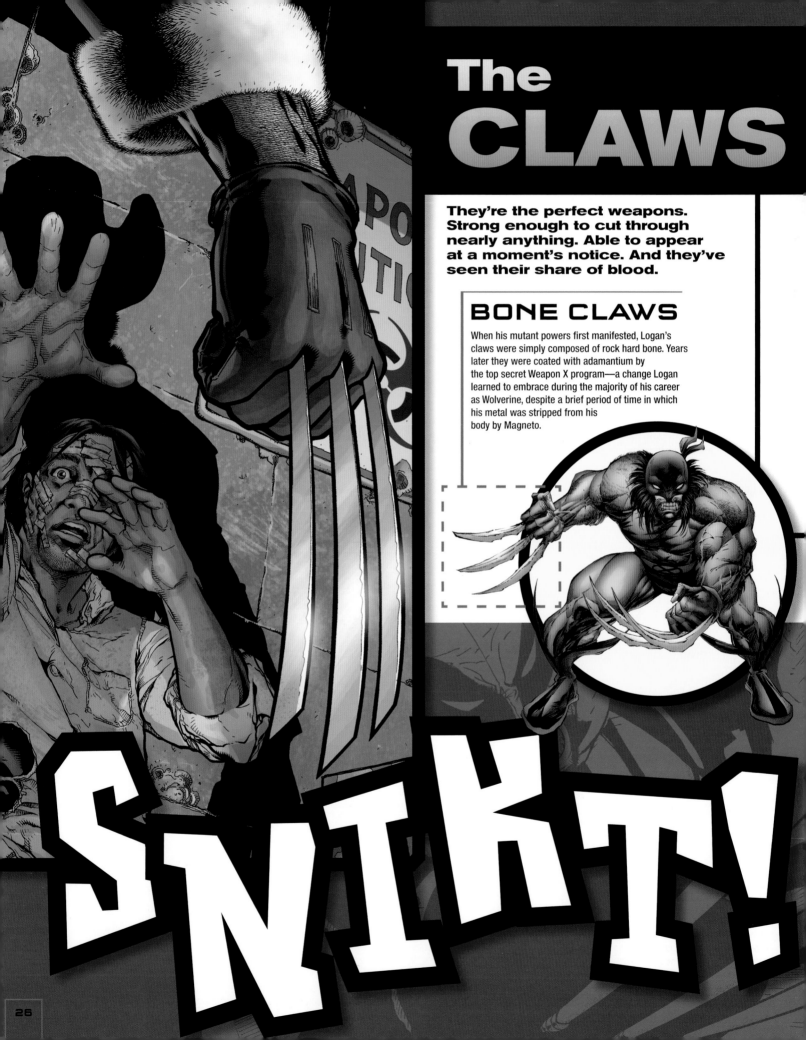

The CLAWS

They're the perfect weapons. Strong enough to cut through nearly anything. Able to appear at a moment's notice. And they've seen their share of blood.

BONE CLAWS

When his mutant powers first manifested, Logan's claws were simply composed of rock hard bone. Years later they were coated with adamantium by the top secret Weapon X program—a change Logan learned to embrace during the majority of his career as Wolverine, despite a brief period of time in which his metal was stripped from his body by Magneto.

SNIKT!

Laced with the near-unbreakable steel alloy, adamantium, Wolverine's claws can cut through virtually anything. This, combined with Wolverine's enhanced mutant strength and heavy adamantium skeleton, means that he has rarely met a target he couldn't slice—even the solid metal of a gun barrel is no contest for the mutant's claws.

The only exception to this rule is adamantium itself. Adamantium is impervious even to other adamantium, and Wolverine's previous attempts at disproving this fact have only served to send his claws back into his arms, causing him immense pain in the process.

CUTTING POWER

WHIFF

SLAAAAAA... ...AAASSHHH

Logan's claws can't slice Silver Samurai's mystic blade, but they can easily penetrate his flesh.

LEARNING CURVE

Though handy in a fight, Wolverine's claws took some getting used to. When not extended, the claws rest in Logan's forearm, and are almost undetectable. In fact, there have been several times in Logan's life when, after being brainwashed, he has been unaware of even possessing his claws in the first place. Back in 1963, during Logan's time with the CIA's Team X division, he was waiting in a holding facility in Dallas, Texas by order of his boss, the shadowy puppet master known as Romulus. On that occasion, Logan avoided the brainwashing procedure he was supposed to undergo, and in a violent fit of rage, popped his claws, for what seemed to him the first time. Soon after he quit Team X, now once again aware of his status as a mutant.

In order to project his claws, Logan uses a mental command that forces the blades through his skin, actually puncturing his flesh each time they are drawn. Popping his claws causes him a small degree of pain, but it is a short-lived sensation, due to Wolverine's healing factor which causes his skin to quickly mend around the small puncture wounds.

MARTIAL ARTS

In an effort to curb his primitive instincts and develop a more civilized fighting method, Logan spent many of his past years abroad, studying various martial arts and fighting techniques. When traveling through China as a merchant marine, Logan attracted the interest of Ogun, a master of martial arts who invited Logan to join his dojo in Kanazawa, Japan, an offer Logan accepted years later. Not content with the teachings of just one master, Logan also studied under master Bando Suboro as well as many other mentors over the years.

Throughout his training, Wolverine always possessed an affinity for bladed weapons.

Logan is a master of precise technique, though he rarely displays this quality in a fight.

SPECIAL SKILLS

• Expert at most unarmed traditional fighting styles, including ju-jitsu, judo, karate, escrima, muay thai, and kali
• Master of the samurai sword
• Master of the *bokken*, a wooden practice sword
• Expert with the machete and other wide knives
• CIA advanced training in espionage and surveillance
• Expert with a crossbow
• A crack shot with most types of firearms

SENSES

A natural-born hunter, Wolverine is endowed with enhanced senses. He utilizes his senses together in order to locate his prey, giving him the tracking ability of a bloodhound.

SIGHT
Wolverine's sight is much more acute than a normal human's, allowing him to see targets at great distances. He also possesses enhanced night vision.

SMELL
Logan often relies on his magnified sense of smell to detect the presence of people nearby, recognizing the particular scents of those he has met in the past.

HEARING
Aware of a predator's location from the slightest rustling in the surrounding brush, Wolverine's intensified hearing also enables him to eavesdrop on others' conversations.

TASTE
Presumably, Logan also enjoys a heightened sense of taste. However he rarely remarks on this ability, not seeming to mind even if his meat is served to him raw.

Though not his style these days, Logan has amassed much experience with firearms.

WEAPONS

Wolverine has felt a kinship with sharp objects ever since his claws first emerged from the back of his hands during his youth. Since his mind has often been tampered with, making his memories of past events inaccessible to him, it was only natural for Logan to adopt the use of similar blades during the periods of his life when he was not aware that he in fact possessed his claws. Also during these times, Logan has become adept at handling a variety of guns. However he has never showed the same level of inborn appreciation for firearms as he has felt toward a sword or dagger.

SNFFF

"THE EQUIVALENT OF AN OLYMPIC GYMNAST DOING A GOLD MEDAL ROUTINE WHILE SIMULTANEOUSLY BEATING FOUR CHESS COMPUTERS IN HIS HEAD!"

FORGE DURING DANGER ROOM TRAINING SESSION

LANGUAGES

Wolverine's extensive travels during his long lifetime have led him to become fluent in many different languages apart from English, including Japanese, Russian, Chinese, Cheyenne, Lakota, and Spanish. He also has a passing knowledge of French, Thai, and Vietnamese.

Regardless of the tough guy image he likes to maintain, Wolverine is an avid reader. *Walden, or Life in the Woods* by Henry Thoreau is one of his favorite books.

WOLVIE'S WIT AND WISDOM

Wolverine's dry sense of humor reveals a lifetime of hard knocks and training in the ways of the eastern world. His one-liners range from the flippant to the philosophical.

"The day I quit fightin' is the day I die."

"I'm the best there is at what I do. But what I do best isn't very nice"

"This wilderness has bite. It has claws. So what—so do I."

"They should have stamped 'Loser' on your forehead when you were born."

"I hear ya don't like mutants. Well we don't much like you!"

"A man comes at me with his fists, I'll meet him with fists. But if he pulls a gun —or threatens people I'm protectin'— then I got no sympathy for him."

"I said huntin' honeybunch—I said nothin' about killin'. It takes no skill t'kill."

"I never used my claws on someone who hadn't tried to kill me first."

"Just think how I might've turned out. I might've wound up a pastry chef."

"We're heroes... We're supposed to stand for something. We're supposed to play by the rules. Because if we don't, why should anybody?"

"I'm the best there is at a couple of things in this world... but what we just did ain't one of them."
Wolverine to Atsuko

Little Girl: "Are You Spider Man?"
Logan: "No darlin'… Spider Man is a sissy."

"I SHOULD HATE MYSELF WHEN I GET LIKE THIS. EVERYTHING GOES RED."

"Let's just say I'm a fast healer."

"I've done a lotta bad things in my life. More than most folks. But then, I've lived a lot longer than most folks."

"Who won? Musta been me, 'cause I'm still breathing..."

"I leave him with his honor. I've got no use for it."

"Human being's an animal, bub—though most animals probably wouldn't take that... as much of a compliment."

"Ninety percent of accidents happen at home, bub."

"I know what you're thinkin', punk. Question is: 'Can I get Wolverine before he turns me into shish-kabob with those claws?'"

"He's in perfect condition. I'm not. I figure that makes us even."

"I lost control. I feel sick. I feel great."

"Funny thing about this mutant healing factor o' mine... it sure doesn't cancel out any of the pain."

"Place still smells the same... just cleaner. Less bloody. But that's probably 'cause I haven't been here in so long."

"...And if you're looking for death... you've come to the right place."

"HE'S BIG AN' MEAN—A ROGUE GRIZZLY BEAR. NO MORE FEARSOME— OR DEADLY—CREATURE EXISTS ON EARTH. 'CEPT ME."

Wolverine to Professor X:
"Thought this was the Danger Room. Oughtta rename it, or you could be sued for fake advertisin'."

"I'M THE BEST THERE IS AT WHAT I DO. BUT WHAT I DO BEST ISN'T SHOPPING."

"Maybe I don't *like* hospitals. Last time, I was on an operatin' table, it didn't turn out so well.

"Mine'll grow back. Yours, on the other hand..."

Does Wolverine have WEAKNESSES?

At first glace he seems to be the ultimate fighter, a natural born scrapper devoid of any Achilles' heel. But despite appearances, Wolverine is not immortal, and it is said that a dire injury could kill him, especially now that his healing factor has been weakened after his encounter with the Angel of Death. However, while there are several elements in the world that could easily bring about his end, it is also believed that even Logan could not recover from decapitation.

THE MURAMASA BLADE

During one the blackest days of Logan's past he gave in to his anger and paid a visit to Muramasa, an ancient Japanese master of the dark arts. With the feral mutant's consent, Muramasa molded the brutal hatred inside of Logan into an actual object, a blade able to cause permanent injury to even Logan's hide. Possessing mystic properties, the Muramasa Blade can negate Logan's healing factor, and cause him lasting injury, or even death.

CARBONADIUM

Created by the Soviets in an attempt to duplicate adamantium, carbonadium is a tough, yet malleable metal which gives off a radioactive aura. During his time as an agent for the mastermind Romulus, Logan ingested carbonadium, and his body's healing factor was negated, making him no more powerful than any other mortal man. With villains such as Omega Red possessing carbonadium tentacles, Wolverine is constantly on the alert for this dangerous alloy.

MAGNETISM

Probably his most obvious weakness, magnetism has taken its toll on Wolverine during more than one encounter. Since his skeleton was bonded with adamantium, Logan has proven fairly ineffectual when battling magnetic-powered villains, particularly the mutant Magneto. Instead, Wolverine often finds himself tossed around like a rag doll at the whim of his opponent, Magneto even using his abilities on one occasion to rip the adamantium from Logan's bones.

MEMORIES and RAGE!

There is more than one way to skin a Wolverine. As many of his villains can attest, Logan is also susceptible to a subtler form of attack. With a past rich in mind manipulations and brainwashings, Logan's head has been a virtual stomping ground for many of his adversaries. With his memories ripe for the picking and altering, Logan can often be stopped dead in his tracks with a psychic attack, especially one that dredges up painful memories or perverts the few cherished recollections that he still possesses.

Perhaps the greatest weakness Wolverine possesses is his limited control over his emotions. When his patience is at and end, or when he has received an injury that wounds him too deeply, Logan's mind snaps into a state of frenzy. This uncontrollable berserker rage grips him on a primal level, and reduces his actions to pure instinct. Without control of himself, Wolverine becomes like a wild animal and therefore greatly susceptible to enemies who rely mainly on their wits.

Logan has always lived a lonely, tortured life.

WOLVERINE IN *Love*

Having lived for over a century, Wolverine has had several lifetimes' worth of romances. But nearly every one, long or short, has ended in heartbreak.

After discovering that his intended, Mariko, was married to someone else, Wolverine had a brief fling with Yukio. But the impetuous daredevil proved too much—even for him.

Ladies' Man

Despite being the runt of the litter, Wolverine still manages to attract more than his fair share of women. Perhaps they are attracted to his confidence and brute strength, or even by the natural pheromones he emits. Whatever the reason, the many women who have touched Logan's heart were all able to look past his apparently crude nature and gruff attitude and find the gentle soul that resides beneath.

Perhaps Wolverine's greatest love was the largely unrequited romance he shared with former X-Man Jean Grey. Jean was usually involved with teammate Cyclops while Wolverine knew her, but Logan stole a kiss from her more than once.

When demonic presences took over Manhattan, Logan's wicked side got the better of both him and Miss Grey.

A Madripoor crime boss and a business associate of Logan's, Tyger Tiger was partial to Wolvie's rough-hewn charm. The two enjoyed a romantic evening together every so often.

At one time, Wolverine had an on-off affair with tricksy, shape-shifting Mystique.

When ATF agent Cassie Lathrop became obsessed with Wolverine, the two had a brief affair. It ended when Logan's past came back to haunt him.

In return for saving his life, he married his longtime foe Viper, a union that helped stabilize the nation of Madripoor.

Wolverine and Amir first met during the Super Hero Civil War. The two enjoyed a whirlwind romance before her untimely death at the hands of an agent of Scimitar.

Wolverine and Storm once shared a kiss on the battlefield, convinced they were at death's door; however their relationship never developed beyond strong friendship.

When Wolverine visited the Savage Land years ago, he met the native Gahck, and the two had a brief affair that may have resulted in the birth of a child.

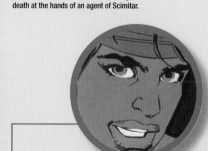

Back before World War II, Wolverine and Seraph, the unscrupulous former owner of Madripoor's Princess Bar, became lovers. Years later, she died at Sabretooth's hands.

Wolverine has no problem finding love, but keeping it is another matter. His trail of lost loves ensures that he remains a lonely and tortured soul.

Love Kills

Wolverine's curse is that nearly every woman he falls in love with dies a violent death. From his childhood love Rose, to Silver Fox, the Native American with whom he spent arguably his happiest moments; from Janet, a fellow operative he loved in the days before World War I, to the Native, a fellow survivor of the Weapon X program, each woman died tragically and without cause. A sinister mind was behind it all, a shadowy figure going by the name Romulus, who was manipulating Wolverine's life for his own twisted agenda.

Mariko

Wolverine and Mariko Yashida, a wealthy Japanese businesswoman with ties to organized crime, carried on a long-distance relationship for years during Wolverine's early time with the X-Men. They were even once engaged, but fate continually kept them apart, separating them either by location, honor, or the interference of a third party. Though Wolverine held the Yashida Blade as her clan's prized warrior, Mariko was determined not to marry him until she had cleaned up her family's criminal enterprises, a feat she only accomplished on her deathbed

After Wolverine killed her evil father, Lord Shingen, he and Mariko were free to get married. However, their union was delayed by the criminal Mastermind, and then later by a debt of honor Mariko felt she owed to her future husband.

FRIENDS & ALLIES

Wolverine's not really a social sort of animal. If his childhood taught him anything, it was to build a wall around his emotions, and never trust anyone. But Wolverine has lived a long life, and from time to time he has let his guard slip. Over the years he has created everything from dedicated lasting friendships, to the bond found only between loyal brothers-in-arms. And today, just as there are many dangerous men and women who consider Wolverine their enemy, there are nearly as many who are proud to call him their friend.

NIGHTCRAWLER

Just as Logan was able to see beyond Kurt Wagner's frightening exterior to the hero that lay beneath, so too was Nightcrawler able to look past Wolverine's gruff manner. Wolverine and Nightcrawler quickly became friends during their original tenure with the X-Men, and Kurt even volunteered to join Logan on an excursion back to Canada. Even after Nightcrawler became a priest, the two remained close—Logan always knowing he has a sounding board if he needs to get something off his chest.

YUKIO

Although not much is known about the past of Wolverine's one-time lover, Yukio, the feral mutant trusts her implicitly and even asked her to serve as a guardian to his ward, Amiko. Although she has turned away from her former life as an assassin and mercenary, Yukio still manages to find her way into more than enough trouble.

AMIKO

Having witnessed the tragic death of Amiko's mother in Japan, Wolverine agreed to watch over the young girl, accepting her as his ward. But with his dangerous life as an X-Man proving an inappropriate environment for a foster father, Logan soon arranged for his lover Mariko to take care of Amiko, followed by Yukio, after Mariko's death.

PUCK

Although Wolverine and Puck know each other from their days with the Canadian Super Hero team Alpha Flight, the relationship between these two fishing buddies stems back much further, to before the Spanish Civil War. Puck was not always so short in stature, but, despite his height, he has always been good in a fight—a plus when drinking at a pub with Logan.

TYGER TIGER

After an encounter with cyborg villains the Reavers changed her life forever, Jessan Hoan decided to become Madripoor's newest crime boss Tyger Tiger—a position Wolverine let her keep as long as she avoided dealing in drugs. Today, Wolverine and Tyger Tiger maintain their bond as trusted allies, with the benefit of the occasional romantic fling.

VINDICATOR

If Logan had had his way, he and Heather Hudson—the Super Hero known as the Vindicator— would have been much more than friends. After all, it was Heather who discovered him roaming the Canadian wild, and Heather who held him until he regained his humanity. Unfortunately, Heather did not feel the same way, and Logan had to settle for her friendship.

NICK FURY

Nick Fury first met Logan during Operation: Blueboy in World War II. They continued to work together many times after the war, both keeping active as intelligence agents for their respective nations. So when Fury became the head of the world peacekeeping organization SHIELD, it was no surprise when he asked Wolverine for help on the occasional mission.

HAVOK

Alex Summers and Logan have not fought alongside each other as X-Men for anywhere near as long as Wolverine and Havok's brother Scott, and they have also never found themselves competing over the affections of a girl. Instead, the two would settle for a beer, a good bar fight, and the occasional road trip to Mexico.

AGENT ZERO

Formerly called Maverick when he and Logan were members of the CIA-sponsored Team X, Christoph Nord changed his name to Agent Zero when he was genetically modified by the Weapon X program. Later losing his powers on M-day, Nord is nonetheless still viewed with such respect by Logan that Logan even placed the deadly carbonadium synthesizer in his care for a time.

JESSICA DREW

Although she has had a lengthy career as Spider-Woman, Jessica Drew didn't become friends with Wolverine until she moved to the Asian island of Madripoor. Working there as a private investigator, she would often partner with Logan and later both heroes served as members of the New Avengers.

ELSIE-DEE AND ALBERT

Artificial beings crafted in the labs of inventor Donald Pierce, Elsie-Dee and Albert were created as the perfect weapons against Wolverine. Appearing as a Wolverine duplicate, Albert was meant to lure Logan into a fight, while the innocent-looking Elsie-Dee self-destructed. However, both androids developed a moral center, and became staunch allies of their intended target.

CAROL DANVERS

Wolverine and Carol Danvers, the woman known today in the Super Hero set as Ms. Marvel, have had a long relationship that dates back to Logan's espionage days. Logan first met Carol when she and Nick Fury rescued him from an attacking pack of Hydra agents during a visit to Washington. The two later flew a mission together to gather intelligence on the Russians.

THE HUNTER IN DARKNESS

The legendary wild beast called the Hunter in Darkness first met Logan in the Canadian wild soon after the feral mutant escaped the Weapon X facility. After freeing the albino beast from a bear trap, Logan stumbled away in the snow, unaware that he had made a new ally who would help him save a young woman from an attacker years later.

SHEATHE THOSE CLAWS, WOLVERINE, OR SO HELP ME --

-- MY NEXT OPTIC BLAST GOES DOWN YOUR THROAT!

I'VE JUST ABOUT HAD IT WITH YOUR "MAD KILLER" ACT PAL.

IT'S NO ACT LEADER-MAN--

-AN' IF YOU DON'T BELIEVE ME, KEEP PUSHIN'!

TEAM PLAYER

He likes to think of himself as a lone wolf. But as Logan is well aware from his own childhood in the Canadian wild, wolves tend to work best in a pack. Despite himself, Logan has been a team player since his debut, even though he constantly finds himself at odds with many of his colleagues. In his long life, Wolverine has served with the Canadian military, various government agencies, and many Super Hero teams. Even on solo mission, Wolverine has a tendency to attract partners, from sidekicks Jubilee and Kitty Pryde, to team-ups with other people of the Super Hero ilk like Spider-Man and Captain America. Wolverine has even been brainwashed into teaming with the terrorist organization Hydra, as well as into joining in with the evil mutant Apocalypse as one of his Horsemen. It seems being a team player is in Logan's blood, whether he likes to think so or not.

X-Men

Above all else, Wolverine is first and foremost an X-Men member. Truly believing in Professor Charles Xavier's vision of a peaceful coexistence between mutants and mankind, Wolverine will make any sacrifice for his fellow mutant teammates.

New Avengers

When fate forced Wolverine to team up with Captain America, Iron Man, Spider-Man and others on an adventure in the Savage Land, he soon found himself accepting membership into the world's premier Super Hero team.

X-Force

Team X

In this CIA-sponsored strike force, Logan's mind was manipulated by the Weapon X program, so much so that he willingly teamed with his arch foe Sabretooth, as well as his former love Silver Fox, among other shady characters.

Alpha Flight

Wolverine was the first recruit to this Canadian Super Hero team, brought into the fold by James MacDonald Hudson. Wolverine's tenure with the Flight was short however, as he soon quit in order to join the X-Men.

Other Teams

Logan has been a part of many other groups over the years, including serving as one of the rotating members in Dr. Strange's Secret Defenders, as well as spending a short stint in a new incarnation of the Fantastic Four.

X-Force

X-Force

Wolverine recently joined this covert mutant strike team as their field leader, under the overall supervision of the team's founder, Cyclops. Serving on X-Force is second nature to Logan, as their deadly tactics allow him to really cut loose.

PARTNERS

He lives in a world packed with mutants and superhumans, so it's only natural that Wolverine would cross paths with other heroes now and again. Although often reluctant to allow anyone else to join in on one of his violent escapades, Logan also recognizes that there are some jobs that require an extra set of helping hands.

SPIDER-MAN

Logan and Peter Parker have almost nothing in common. With his way of finding humor in almost every situation, Spider-Man's personality is the opposite of Wolverine's tough, no-nonsense persona. So how the two have managed to team-up on dozens of occasions is anyone's guess.

As Super Heroes are wont to do, Logan and Spidey have often started their missions together with a fight. During the period in the X-Men's career where the world at large believed them to be dead, Spidey attacked Wolverine on a rooftop, thinking the man in costume was an imposter. However, Parker discovered his mistake fairly quickly, and soon he and Logan were pairing up in order to rescue a little girl from a group of evil mutants.

Despite their fundamental differences, over the years Wolverine and Spider-Man have developed a mutual respect for one another. On one occasion Peter even invited his mutant ally over for dinner after a particularly harrowing SHIELD mission.

THE PUNISHER

After Frank Castle's family was killed by members of New York's mafia, he started a brutal war against the city's underworld. Calling himself the Punisher, he killed any criminal dumb enough to cross his path. With such a single-minded vendetta, Castle has caught Logan in his crosshairs several times, and the two troubled Super Heroes only combine forces when given no other choice. This was the case when they encountered each other in the South American jungle outside a town known as Erewhon. On a normal day, the two seem much more comfortable at each other's throats, and over the course of their many fights, the Punisher has run Logan over with a steamroller, shot him with a bazooka, and even sicced the Hulk on his feral adversary.

KITTY PRYDE

When Kitty Pryde first came to the Xavier School for Gifted Youngsters she was a wide-eyed innocent young girl, still struggling to master her newly discovered power to pass through solid matter. But Charles Xavier, the school's headmaster and founder of the secret Super Hero team the X-Men, had plans for his shy new student. Pairing Kitty with the battle-hardened veteran Wolverine, Xavier unwittingly awarded Logan a faithful and unswerving sidekick.

Although at first he found Kitty a hindrance and her presence annoying, Wolverine soon grew fond of the young girl's optimistic attitude, and began to view her as a sort of surrogate daughter. As Kitty continued to develop her crime fighting skills, she accompanied Logan on many different missions, including a recruitment drive to locate a new mutant, one of Wolverine's birthday brawls versus Sabretooth, and even a trip to the bizarre Wundagore Mountain.

GHOST RiDER

When an attack at a Madripoor bar led Wolverine to Manhattan, he found himself partnering Danny Ketch—the cursed supernatural avenger known as Ghost Rider—in order to take down a villain named Deathwatch. Soon after, the two joined forces with Spider-Man and the Hulk to form a brief incarnation of the Fantastic Four.

ELEKTRA

Wolverine has teamed up with the female assassin Elektra many times over the years. They formed an unbreakable bond when she helped coach him back to his normal self after a battle with the demented mutant Genesis left him in a primitive state. Logan even became a sounding board for her when she attempted to restart her life as a dancer. But the two lost touch when Elektra fell back into her old ways and resumed her career as an assassin.

BEN GRiMM

Before Ben Grimm was bathed in cosmic rays and became the Fantastic Four member known as Thing, he and Logan partnered on a few occasions, while Logan worked for Canadian intelligence. On their first meeting, Grimm flew his mutant companion to Washington. On their second, the two piloted a spy plane into Russian airspace.

HULK

The Hulk and Wolverine have fought each other as many times as they have fought alongside each other and have developed a mutual animosity, resulting in anything from fairly harmless pranks to extreme violence. Once, when the Hulk visited Madripoor, Wolverine began to torment his old rival by immediately arranging for the behemoth's expensive clothing collection to be replaced with dozens of pairs of embarrassing purple pants instead.

GAMBiT

Logan and Gambit have much experience fighting side by side while serving together on the X-Men, but the two have also enjoyed a few missions without their other mutant cohorts. They once journeyed to England to combat the female mutant Mastermind, and her partner, Arcade.

JUBiLEE

Orphan Jubilation Lee, aka Jubilee, was a California mallrat with pyrotechnic abilities who helped rescue Logan from an attack by the cyborg gang known as the Reavers. Using her street survival instincts as well as her mutant pyrotechnic displays to get the injured Wolverine out of harm's way, she soon became a fixture in Logan's life and accompanied him on dozens of adventures as his sidekick.

Wolverine's enemies

SABRETOOTH

Perhaps Wolverine's oldest and most hated enemy, Victor Creed became a lifetime foe when he murdered Logan's Native American lover Silver Fox. After that, the two spent years at each other's throats, in a conflict drawn out by their evenly matched mutant physiques and healing factors, until Logan finally managed to slay his rival.

LADY DEATHSTRIKE

Daughter of a shamed kamikaze pilot and scientist, Yuriko Oyama became obsessed with the adamantium bonding process, a formula she felt was created from notes stolen from her deceased father. Because Logan's body was laced with that very metal, he became the focus of her hatred.

WILD CHILD

Like Wolverine, Kyle Gibney, led a life as an unwilling guinea pig and later overcame his feral instincts to serve as a member of Alpha Flight. However, under the influence of Romulus, Wild Child recently succumbed to his darker side.

LORD SHINGEN

The father of Wolverine's beloved, Mariko Yashida, and the head of the ancient Yashida Clan, Lord Shingen battled with Logan to the death over the corrupt man's crimes. Although Logan triumphed at the time, Shingen was mysteriously resurrected, renewing his old campaign against the man who took his life.

SHIVA

A series of robots designed by the Weapon X program, the Shiva units were meant as a defense system against surviving test subjects. With an adaptive program that never falls prey to the same method of defeat twice, the Shiva androids proved to be dangerous adversaries for Wolverine when he accidentally activated them.

SILVER SAMURAI

The mutant son of Lord Shingen, Kenuichio Harada possesses the ability to focus his body's energy through his sword, making his blade able to cut through most any substance. He hated Wolverine for his involvement in the Yashida Clan. This hatred deepened when Wolverine severed his hand.

OMEGA RED

Serial killer turned super-soldier by the Russian Government, Arkady Gregorivich was trained by the KGB to be the ultimate warrior. Arkady was outfitted with carbonadium tentacles in each of his forearms. The tentacles served as conduits for his formidable natural powers, which included an energy-draining "mutant death factor." As Omega Red, Arkady has clashed with Wolverine many times.

EPSILON RED

Another super-soldier developed by the Russian government, Epsilon Red's body was altered to withstand exposure to the extremes of outer space. Though Logan originally met Red on an assignment organized by the CIA to assassinate him, the next time he crossed paths with the misunderstood multi-tentacled mutant, he greeted him as an ally.

With a fuse to match his stature, Wolverine's temper has gotten him into many scraps in his lifetime. And after amassing over a century's worth of fights to his credit, Logan has racked up a small army's share of enemies, many of whom, like an incurable virus, keep coming back time and time again to plague the diminutive mutant hero.

BLOODSCREAM

Also known as Bloodsport, the vampiric Bloodscream possesses the ability to suck the life force out of his prey, merely by touch. Having encountered Wolverine several times during his century-spanning lifetime, Bloodscream is a frequent partner of the super-strong Roughouse, the pair often working as hired muscle.

DAKEN

The son of Logan and his wife Itsu, Daken was presumed dead by his father when a pregnant Itsu was slain by the Winter Soldier. Only years later, when Daken had been conditioned by Romulus to hate his birth father, did Wolverine and son finally meet.

CYBER

Originally Logan's drill sergeant back when he trained with a shadowy outfit of killers during his brainwashed days working for Romulus, Silas Burr continued to haunt Wolverine as the adamantium-armored Cyber, a twisted, super-strong sadist with a healing factor and poison-tipped finger claws.

ROUGHOUSE

Hailing from the fabled home of the Norse gods, Asgard, the man-mountain named Roughouse first came into contact with Wolverine in Madripoor as hired muscle. Although they have teamed up on occasion, Roughouse and Wolverine are more commonly found trading thunderous punches.

GORGON

A member of the criminal organizations Hydra and the Hand, Tomi Shishido possessed the mutant ability to turn people into stone with just a glance. Extremely intelligent, and possessing superhuman stamina, speed, and strength, the Gorgon proved more than a match for Wolverine and even succeeded in killing, resurrecting, and subsequently brainwashing his feral opponent.

WENDIGO

A mystical albino brute normally found wandering the Canadian wilderness, the super-strong Wendigo is the result of a magical curse. Several people have been turned into the cannibalistic monster, and many of them have faced Wolverine, his relationship with the creature dating back to one of his first missions for Canada's Department H.

ROMULUS

With a past as shrouded in mystery as any enemy Wolverine has faced, little is known about Romulus, save his name and that he stems from the lupine order of mutants. Whatever his motivations, Romulus has spent the last century of his ancient life manipulating and controlling Logan's life.

OGUN

An old friend and sensei of Logan's, Ogun trained the future Wolverine years ago in the ways of the martial arts. Later, when Ogun strayed from the path of honor, the two met again when Kitty Pryde succumbed to Ogun's brainwashing, a slight Wolverine was not prepared to ignore.

OMEGA RED

Like his archenemy Wolverine, Arkady Gregorivich's past is something of a mystery. A captured serial killer handed over to the KGB, Gregorivich was to be the ultimate weapon for the communist agenda. Codenamed Omega Red, Gregorivich's transformation into a super-soldier was interrupted when Wolverine and his teammates of the CIA-sponsored Team X, Sabretooth and Maverick, sabotaged the operation by stealing the Carbonadium Synthesizer, the tool instrumental in the soldier's creation, and freed double agent Janice Hollenbeck. However Sabretooth was given another mission on the orders of Romulus, the mysterious figure who was secretly manipulating Wolverine's life. Sabretooth's attempting to recruit Omega Red to Romulus's cause, ended in an impromptu battle. Logan secured the Synthesizer, and the trio managed to escape, at the cost of Hollenbeck's life (something Sabretooth had planned from the start, in a play to keep Wolverine in check).

CAUGHT UP
Omega Red possesses the ability to sap a person's life energy, his carbonadium tentacles serving as the conduits for this mutant power. And since carbonadium cancels out Wolverine's healing factor, this makes Omega Red twice as deadly to him.

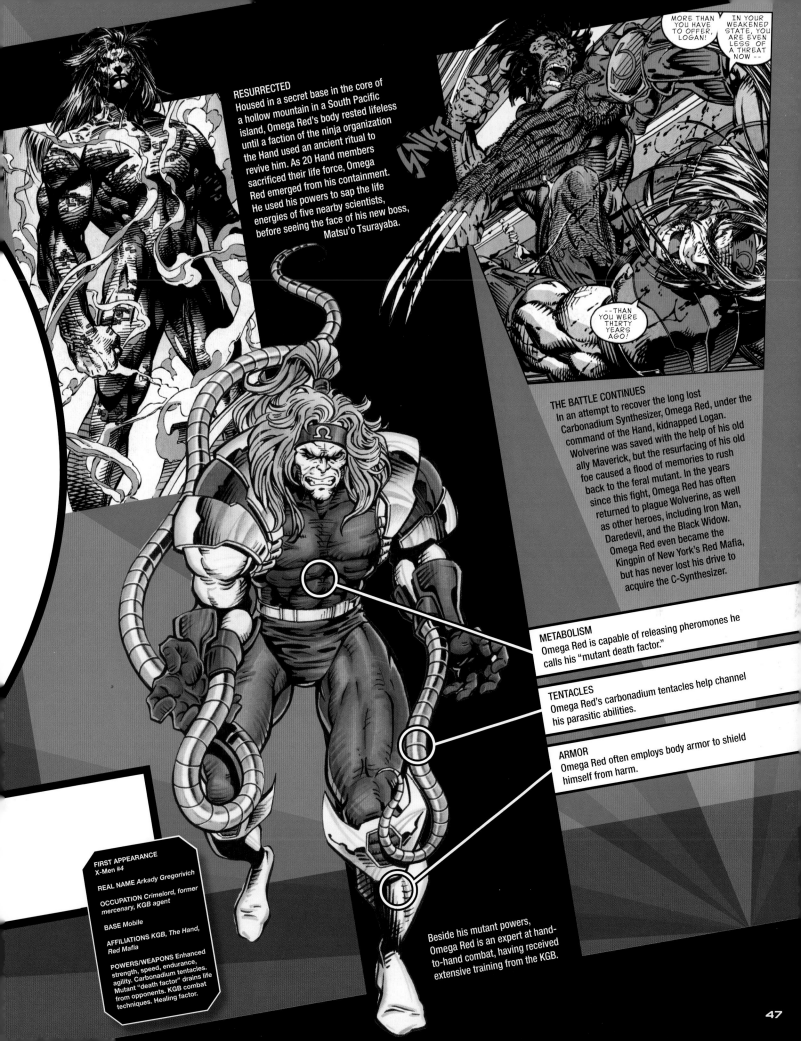

RESURRECTED
Housed in a secret base in the core of a hollow mountain in a South Pacific island, Omega Red's body rested lifeless until a faction of the ninja organization the Hand used an ancient ritual to revive him. As 20 Hand members sacrificed their life force, Omega Red emerged from his containment. He used his powers to sap the life energies of five nearby scientists, before seeing the face of his new boss, Matsu'o Tsurayaba.

MORE THAN YOU HAVE TO OFFER, LOGAN! IN YOUR WEAKENED STATE, YOU ARE EVEN LESS OF A THREAT NOW --

--THAN YOU WERE THIRTY YEARS AGO!

THE BATTLE CONTINUES
In an attempt to recover the long lost Carbonadium Synthesizer, Omega Red, under the command of the Hand, kidnapped Logan. Wolverine was saved with the help of his old ally Maverick, but the resurfacing of his old foe caused a flood of memories to rush back to the feral mutant. In the years since this fight, Omega Red has often returned to plague Wolverine, as well as other heroes, including Iron Man, Daredevil, and the Black Widow. Omega Red even became the Kingpin of New York's Red Mafia, but has never lost his drive to acquire the C-Synthesizer.

METABOLISM
Omega Red is capable of releasing pheromones he calls his "mutant death factor."

TENTACLES
Omega Red's carbonadium tentacles help channel his parasitic abilities.

ARMOR
Omega Red often employs body armor to shield himself from harm.

FIRST APPEARANCE X-Men #4

REAL NAME Arkady Gregorivich

OCCUPATION Crimelord, former mercenary, KGB agent

BASE Mobile

AFFILIATIONS KGB, The Hand, Red Mafia

POWERS/WEAPONS Enhanced strength, speed, endurance, agility. Carbonadium tentacles. Mutant "death factor" drains life from opponents. KGB combat techniques. Healing factor.

Beside his mutant powers, Omega Red is an expert at hand-to-hand combat, having received extensive training from the KGB.

CHAPTER **TWO**

The Life of Wolverine

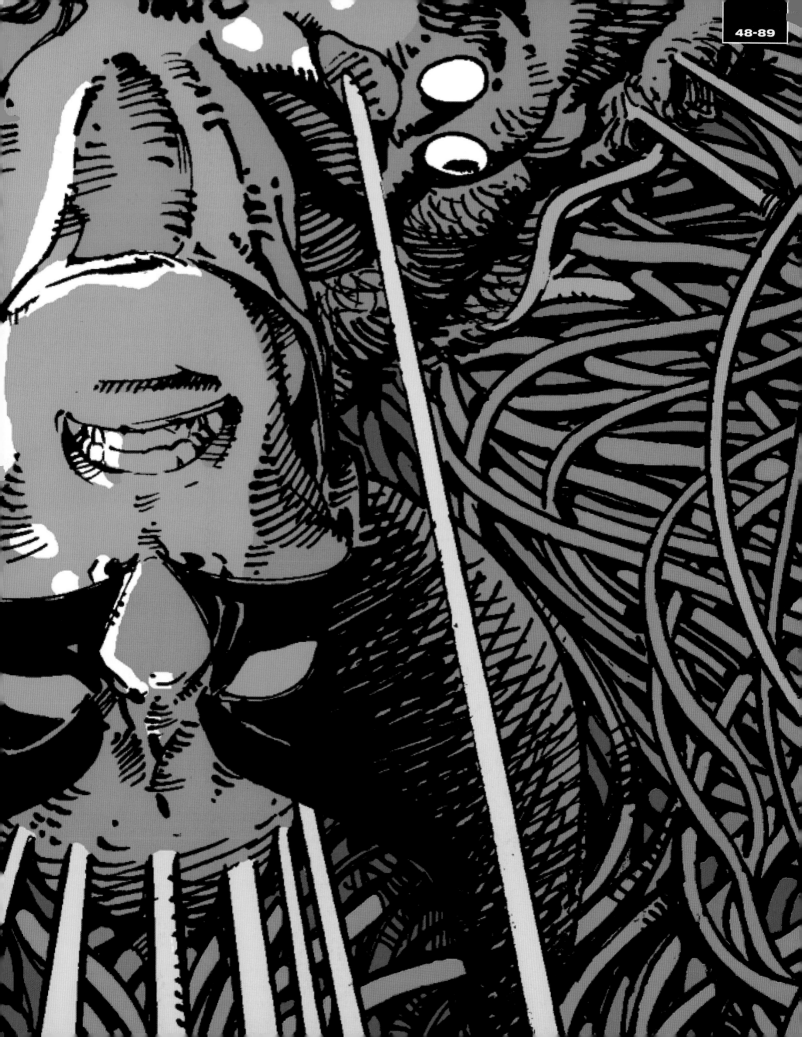

Timeline

James Howlett is born to John and Elizabeth Howlett in Alberta, Canada in the late 1800s.

A sickly child, James befriends Rose, a young servant girl, and Dog, the son of the groundskeeper Thomas Logan.

James discovers his mutant powers when Thomas Logan murders his father. At this time, James's mother also takes her own life.

Rose and James flee the Alberta estate, and head to the Yukon Territory where James adopts the name Logan in order to keep his anonymity. He begins a job working in a quarry. Logan's mutant healing factor helps erase his memories of his parents' traumatic deaths.

Now a young adult, Logan accidentally kills Rose when Dog attacks him. Logan flees into the woods, renouncing his humanity to live like an animal.

Resurfacing into civilization, Logan begins work for the Hudson Bay Company.

Logan meets the Blackfoot tribe and battles a mystical monster called Uncegila. He is referred to as Skunk-Bear by them, a name which translates as Wolverine.

While in Tokyo, Logan is abducted by a man he later realizes was the master manipulator Romulus. At Romulus's request, Logan encounters Sabretooth for the first time when Creed is attacking a prostitute. Logan stops Creed's attack, and Sabretooth swears payback for Logan's interruption.

In the Canadian Rocky Mountains, Logan settles down in a cabin with a Native American woman named Silver Fox. The two live a quiet, happy life until Sabretooth seemingly murders Silver Fox on Logan's birthday.

Logan loses the ensuing fight with Sabretooth and is left in a pit. There he is manipulated by Romulus and Sabretooth into giving in to his anger.

Venturing to Madripoor for the first time, Logan has a romantic liaison with the owner of the Princess Bar, Seraph.

In 1912, Logan is trained in a Canadian covert military camp run by a mysterious man named Hudson.

Logan takes a girlfriend, a fellow operative named Janet. His drill sergeant Silas Burr then kills her on orders from Romulus, sending Logan into an animalistic state. He is retrieved by Sabretooth and Burr, his healing factor and brainwashing making him forget the event.

Logan fights for Canada in World War I in Belgium in 1915. He defeats Lazaer, the angel of death, on the battlefield, and falls into a deep depression.

Mystique and Logan meet in Mexico in 1921 and escape a firing squad to move to Kansas City together. They become lovers, but part ways following a botched bank robbery.

As a merchant marine, Logan travels to Shanghai, China and meets his future mentor, ninja and martial arts Master Ogun.

Logan begins work for the interdimensional firm of Landau, Luckman, and Lake after encountering a mysterious man named Chang.

Logan journeys to Madripoor in 1932 and reunites with Seraph, where he works in her employ as an assassin.

Along with writer Ernest Hemingway and future Alpha Flight member Puck, Logan fights in Spain in 1937 during the Spanish Civil War.

On a mission in the Soviet Union, Logan meets Natalia Romanova, the future Black Widow, for the first time, and begins to train her. He later murders her father.

Back in Japan, Logan trains with Master Ogun, becoming an expert in the martial arts and learning the Japanese language.

Heading back to Madripoor in 1941, Logan meets Captain America for the first time, and the two help rescue Natasha Romanova from Baron Von Strucker.

In 1942, Logan fights once again alongside Captain America, this time in the Italian Alps. There he meets Wild Child for presumably the first time. During World War II, Logan participates in Operation: Blueboy on orders from Seraph and Romulus, and teams up with Captain America, meeting Bucky and Nick Fury for the first time. Cap and Logan part ways as enemies, despite Logan disobeying Romulus's orders in an effort to save Captain America's life.

Later, in Poland, Wolverine is taken prisoner at the Sobibor Nazi death camp, where he successfully torments the installation's various leaders.

In Normandy in 1944, Logan jumps with the 1st Canadian Parachute Division during the D-Day invasion.

In the closing days of World War II, Logan is taken prisoner in a Japanese POW camp. He manages to escape and meets a woman named Atsuko. The two share a passionate night together before Atsuko is murdered and Logan is caught in the explosion of a nuclear bomb dropped on Hiroshima by the Americans in 1945.

Logan travels to Jasmine Falls in Japan at the suggestion of his former sensei, Ogun. There he meets Itsu, and the two fall in love. Logan trains under sensei Bando Suboro.

Itsu and Logan are finally married. After she becomes pregnant with Logan's child, she is murdered by the Winter Soldier. Logan heads to the nearby camp of the ancient Muramasa, and Muramasa creates a sword out of Logan's anger.

Logan is abducted by the Winter Soldier, who is under orders from Romulus to take Logan back to Madripoor.

Having survived the death of his mother, Logan's son Daken is given to a man named Akihira and his wife in Sendai, Japan, in 1946.

In 1953, brainwashed and working again for Romulus, Logan aids in the death of Charles Simpson in Dayton, Ohio, helping to destroy the life of his son Frank, the future villain Nuke.

Logan starts to work for Team X, a CIA-sponsored strike force run by the Weapon X department. His travels take him all over the world on various missions. During this time, Logan is subjected to various fake memory implants, and his past memories are altered.

After his first encounter with the evil Soviet super-soldier Omega Red, Logan quits Team X when Sabretooth murders a female double agent in cold blood in order to teach Logan a lesson.

In 1968, under orders by Romulus, Logan tortures Frank Simpson, finalizing his transformation into the twisted super-soldier called Nuke.

Logan begins solo intelligence work for Canada, and becomes an alcoholic, despite his healing factor, accidentally shooting a fellow agent at the firing range.

Logan is abducted by the secret Weapon X project, and has his skeleton bonded with adamantium, with the intention of making him the perfect killing machine for the government. In a Canadian complex, he is subjected to hundreds of tests and experiments, and has his mind and memories once again tampered with.

Escaping Weapon X in a veritable bloodbath with the help of the Winter Soldier, Logan retreats into the Canadian wild, where he lives like an animal in the forest.

Logan meets the mythical Canadian beast known as the Hunter in Darkness, and frees the creature from a hunter's trap.

In a modest cabin in the Pacific Northwest, Logan begins a life with a female Weapon X escapee known as the Native.

In Canada's Wood Buffalo National Park, Logan is discovered by James and Heather Hudson, the young couple taking Wolverine in and helping him calm down and regain his senses.

Logan enrolls in James Hudson's project, the Canadian government's Department H program. There he is given the codename Weapon X, as well as Wolverine, and adopts a Super Hero uniform to match his new persona.

Despite being a part of Department H, Logan continues his intelligence work for the Canadian government, teaming with other future heroes such as Ben Grimm (later the Thing) and Carol Danvers (later Ms. Marvel).

On a mission for Department H, Wolverine attempts to take down the Hulk, but is interrupted when the two encounter the Wendigo.

Wolverine helps lead Alpha Flight, a band of Canadian Super Heroes, before quitting on unfriendly terms when recruited by Professor X into his X-Men.

On a mission to Krakoa, Wolverine cements his membership with the X-Men and decides to stay with the team on a permanent basis.

Logan falls in love with X-Man Jean Grey after she seemingly dies on a mission and is resurrected as the Phoenix.

Venturing to Japan alongside the X-Men, Logan meets his future love Mariko Yashida for the first time.

The X-Men battle Jean Grey's supposed alter ego the Dark Phoenix, and Wolverine watches as Jean seemingly perishes for a second time.

Logan dons a new brown and tan version of his costume, and then makes peace with his old allies of Alpha Flight.

Mariko journeys to New York, and she and Logan begin a formal courtship that continues for years.

Unable to reach Mariko by phone, Logan travels to Japan and discovers she has been forced to marry another by her cruel, criminal father, Lord Shingen. Mariko's husband and father are killed in the subsequent skirmish, and Logan and Mariko become engaged.

As the X-Men travel to Japan for Logan's wedding ceremony, Mariko calls off the festivities while under the mind control of villain Mastermind. She later regains her true emotions, but still refuses to marry Logan until she has severed all ties to the Yashida's criminal empire.

Logan meets Amiko, and promises her dying mother to watch over the young girl. He soon leaves Amiko in Mariko's care as he returns to the United States.

Again finding himself in Japan, Wolverine kills Ogun when his former sensei tries to brainwash fellow X-Man Kitty Pryde.

Wolverine meets Lady Deathstrike while being paid a visit by Heather Hudson, now a Super Hero in her own right called the Vindicator.

The X-Men face the threat of the Marauders in what would later be known as the Mutant Massacre, providing the setting for one of Wolverine's most brutal battles with Sabretooth.

As the X-Men relocate their base to Australia, faking their deaths, Logan begins to spend much of his time again in Madripoor.

Logan travels to the Savage Land and has a relationship with a native woman named Gahck, their bond seemingly resulting in the birth of a child.

Wolverine is ambushed in Australia by the Reavers and is saved from a torturous death by the young Jubilee.

While in Madripoor, Logan once again tangles with his former drill sergeant Silas Burr, the villain now calling himself Cyber.

Wolverine returns to the Weapon X complex with Jubilee and once again adopts his blue and yellow costume, struggling with his many fake memories.

During another trip to Japan, Logan watches helplessly as his love Mariko is poisoned by the Hand criminal organization. Wolverine kills his love in an act of mercy to ease her suffering.

Logan reunites with some of his former Team X allies and realizes that Silver Fox is still alive, only to watch her die once more at the hands of the vicious Sabretooth.

While storming the Avalon space satellite, the adamantium in Wolverine's body is ripped from his bones by the villain Magneto. Logan barely survives the attack, and from that day forward, is forced to rely on his natural bone claws.

The unbalanced mutant Genesis kidnaps Logan in an attempt to recreate him as a Horseman for the mutant overlord Apocalypse. Attempting to bond adamantium once more to Logan's frame, Genesis reduces Wolverine to a feral state when Logan manages to reject the transfusion.

With the help of the ninja Elektra, Wolverine regains control of his faculties, and regains his human demeanor.

Forced to return to Madripoor, Logan fulfills an old debt to his enemy Viper, marrying her in order to help unite the country's citizens under her rule.

During a trip through time to battle the planet-eating villain Galactus, Wolverine and the X-Men are frozen in stasis. The shape-shifting aliens known as the Skrulls use this opportunity to abduct Logan and replace him with one of their own.

The Skrulls give Wolverine to Apocalypse, where he becomes the evil mutant's brainwashed servant Death, receiving his adamantium back in the process.

With the help of the X-Men, Logan regains control of his mind, and rejects Apocalypse's programming.

In Madripoor, Viper divorces Wolverine in exchange for medical treatment following a clash with the spirit of Logan's old master, Ogun.

Logan returns to Xavier's school in Westchester as a part of the New X-Men. He begins a teaching position there, serving as a rather unusual mentor.

Along with Cyclops and the mysterious Fantomex, Logan invades a Weapons Plus base, learning more about his past traumas.

Wolverine and Jean Grey are trapped in space during a visit to Asteroid M. As they hurtle toward the sun, Logan is forced to kill Jean in order to hasten her death and end her pain. Set free, Jean accesses the Phoenix force, and brings them both back to Earth, only to truly die at the hands of the villain Xorn.

Logan reunites with the Native in their old cabin, only to watch her die at Sabretooth's hands.

Wolverine is killed by the mutant Gorgon during a return visit to Japan, and resurrected under the ninja clan Hand's control. He finally regains his true personality through the help of SHIELD, and slays his former killer.

During an adventure in the Savage Land, Wolverine teams up with several other heroes, unwittingly becoming one of the New Avengers.

The former Avenger Scarlet Witch reforms the world so that mutants are in the majority. Wolverine regains all his lost memories, and retains them even as the world is returned to normal.

Logan sets out to avenge past wrongs, once again garbed in his brown and tan costume. On a quest that brings him into conflict with many of his old enemies, Logan traces his origins, and discovers that his son Daken is still alive.

After an explosion at Stamford, Connecticut, and the subsequent start of the Super Hero Civil War, Logan tracks down Nitro, the villain responsible for the tragedy.

Wolverine joins with the so-called Secret Avengers, helping the group of heroes hide from the Super Hero Registration Act.

Logan kills Sabretooth after discovering their lupine mutant history, and realizing the scope of their connections to the evil manipulator Romulus.

In a battle involving Lazaer and Mariko's resurrected father, Lord Shingen, Logan reclaims a piece of his soul that was missing since Gorgon killed him. His healing powers are severely lessened as a result.

After the events of the Messiah Complex event, Wolverine joins the new X-Men strike force team X-Force as field leader.

Wolverine takes part in fending off the Earth from an invading hoard of Skrulls during the Secret Invasion event.

As a boy, James Howlett grew up in a giant mansion in Alberta, Canada, raised as an only child to solemn parents who were affected deeply by the death of his older brother.

CHILDHOOD FRIENDS

James lived a lonely life. His only friends were Dog, the son of the cruel groundskeeper Logan, and Rose, a young orphan sent to the house by her aunt as a servant. The three became fast companions despite their differences in social status and manners. While Dog was the rough and tumble result of an abusive home, James was a sickly child, often bedridden due to various allergies.

THE ORIGIN

JAMES HOWLETT WAS BORN INTO A TRAGIC FAMILY WITH DARK, LINGERING SECRETS, INCLUDING A DEAD OLDER BROTHER.

JOHN HOWLETT

James's older brother John had died at the tender age of 12 by causes known only to the Howlett family. The young boy's death, however it occurred, proved too much for his mother, and Elizabeth was soon put into a madhouse in order to cope with her grief. When she returned to the estate, she was a shadow of her former self. The only souvenir she possessed of this strange, tragic episode was a set of mysterious claw marks that scarred her back. She locked herself away in her room, not even bothering to visit with her still living son James.

REVENGE

As Thomas Logan fired his shotgun, killing the senior John Howlett in front of the eyes of his son, young James was overcome with a berserker rage. Razor-sharp claws of bone emerged from the backs of his hands for the first time in his life. James charged Logan, accidentally stabbing the killer in the stomach.

BREAKING POINT

Thomas Logan had had enough. The longtime groundskeeper for the Howlett family, he was rumored to have had a torrid affair with the lady of the house, Elizabeth. Logan was finally fired from his position after the violent acts of his son, Dog. Deciding to seize what he considered his own property, Logan and Dog stormed the mansion in an attempt to kidnap Elizabeth, and take a good chunk of the Howlett family fortune as well. Only the timely intervention by Elizabeth's husband and son prevented Logan from seeing his plan through.

"YOU KILLED MY PAPA! I'LL KILL YOU BACK! I'LL KILL YOU!"

Whether caused by the onset of adolescence or a surge of adrenaline, James Howlett's mutant abilities were triggered that night.

After scarring Dog's face with his claws, James fled into the nearby woods with Rose, his senses heightened and his mind in a state of shock. Feeling pity for the helpless boy, who seemed to remember nothing of what had happened, and realizing she would be implicated in the bloodbath, Rose took James and quit their home forever.

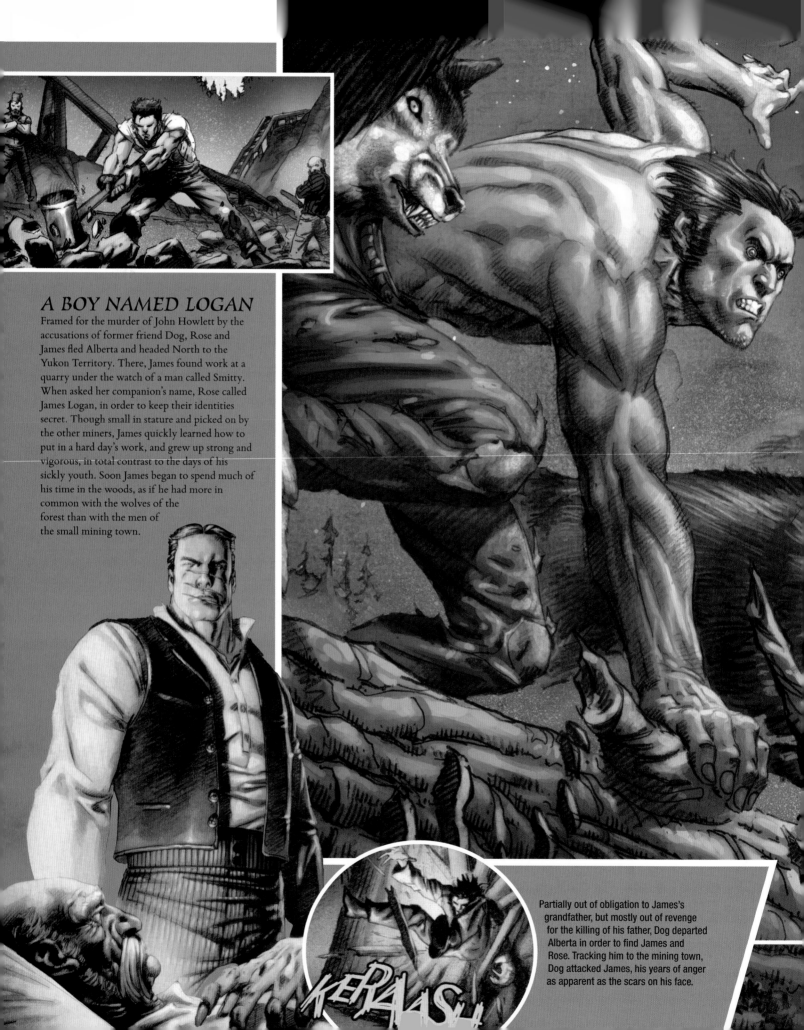

A BOY NAMED LOGAN

Framed for the murder of John Howlett by the accusations of former friend Dog, Rose and James fled Alberta and headed North to the Yukon Territory. There, James found work at a quarry under the watch of a man called Smitty. When asked her companion's name, Rose called James Logan, in order to keep their identities secret. Though small in stature and picked on by the other miners, James quickly learned how to put in a hard day's work, and grew up strong and vigorous, in total contrast to the days of his sickly youth. Soon James began to spend much of his time in the woods, as if he had more in common with the wolves of the forest than with the men of the small mining town.

KERAASH

Partially out of obligation to James's grandfather, but mostly out of revenge for the killing of his father, Dog departed Alberta in order to find James and Rose. Tracking him to the mining town, Dog attacked James, his years of anger as apparent as the scars on his face.

JAMES AND ROSE

Carving out a simple life for themselves, James and Rose lived in a small cabin in the woods. As James worked at the mine and developed into a fine hunter in his spare time, Rose kept a written account of their life in her journal, wishing her childhood friend would open up to her and discuss what had happened on that fateful night back in Alberta. As "Logan" started to become as wild and uncouth as his namesake, fighting with other miners and hunting with the wolves by night, he started to lust after Rose. However Rose began to develop a close relationship with Smitty, who had taken a shine to the pretty young woman. Soon Smitty and Rose decided to be married and move to a new town, putting this hard life behind them. Logan took the news poorly, and took out his frustration in a local barroom cage match. But when pitted against Smitty himself for the grand prize, Logan's feelings for Rose got the better of him and he nobly and deliberately lost the fight in order to ensure that Rose and Smitty would have enough money to begin a new life together.

ROSE'S DEATH

Hearing of Logan's injuries in the cage fight, Rose ran to the bar to make sure he was okay. But Logan was anything but okay. Attacked by Dog after exhausting himself in the cage matches, Logan was pinned by his foe, until memories of his father's murder flooded his mind. Possessed by berserker rage, Logan was about to kill Dog, until Rose stepped between them, trying to protect her childhood friends. Logan's claws pierced her chest and she fell dead. In despair, Logan retreated into the wilderness, abandoning his life and his humanity.

Silver FOX

THE CABIN

He had found civilization again, or his version of it. In a cabin somewhere in the Canadian wilderness, Logan had started a new life for himself: a modest, yet happy existence with a Native American squaw of the Blackfoot tribe named Silver Fox. For the first time in his life, Logan felt truly at peace, his daily routine of hunting and farm chores around the homestead rewarded with the touch of his beautiful young love. But as ever, there were other forces at work in Logan's life. In the shadows lurked manipulative people who desired further control over the powerful young mutant and mold his future as an unfeeling killing machine.

Matters came to a head on Logan's birthday. After Silver Fox sent him into town so she could prepare for the festivities, she was attacked by Wolverine's longtime foe Sabretooth. Apparently under the employ of the enigmatic Romulus, Sabretooth propositioned Silver Fox, forcing himself on her and killing her when she denied him. When Logan returned to his idyllic cabin in the woods, he was greeted by the sight of the corpse of his former lover and a message scrawled in blood on the cabin wall: "Happy Birthday."

She was Wolverine's fondest memory. His days spent in her company were among the happiest of his life. So, of course, it couldn't end well...

FIRST APPEARANCE
Wolverine #10

OCCUPATION *Secret agent, terrorist*

BASE *The Canadian Rockies, unnamed Manhattan Hydra building*

AFFILIATIONS *Hydra, Weapon X, Team X*

POWERS/WEAPONS *Healing factor and age suppressant*

Even Wolverine's best memories of his life with Silver Fox are still tarnished with regret. He frequently obsesses over the things he wishes he had done differently, particularly in the instance when he sensed Sabretooth's presence at the cabin, just hours before Silver Fox's murder.

"SHE'S DEAD!..."

Wolverine carried a tragic burden into town, vengeance on his mnd.

Despite knowing that his old enemy was watching him from afar, Wolverine ignored the brute, wanting to flaunt his happiness in front of his foe—a decision fraught with disastrous consequences.

SABRETOOTH MUST DIE!

Bursting into a local bar with the body of Silver Fox still warm in his arms, Wolverine demanded to know who her killer was. At the bar sat Sabretooth, enjoying a slice of cake and smiling proudly about what he had accomplished. What followed was one of the greatest fights between the two enemies, a bloody, no-holds-barred conflict that continued in the street and then in the surrounding wilderness. Sabretooth knocked Wolverine off a cliff, the two plummeting into a snowy bank. Thinking his enemy dead, Sabretooth stumbled away in triumph. Had he looked back, he would have noticed that his enemy still stirred. Barely alive, Wolverine swore to be avenged on the man who had stolen his perfect life from him.

TEAM X

During his time with the fabled CIA-sponsored Weapon X team called Team X, Logan partnered with his old foe Sabretooth, the man-mountain Mastodon, the teleporting John Wraith, the young gun Maverick, and none other than Silver Fox herself. Although Wolverine didn't recall his time serving with Team X until years after the fact, what he did remember didn't square with his memories of life in his quaint Canadian cabin.

The Return

Silver Fox's fate proved stranger than Wolverine could have imagined. She had not died on that fateful day in the Canadian wilderness. In fact, his former love was still very much alive.

The blame could be placed squarely on the clandestine Weapon X program that had birthed Team X. To better control their subjects, Weapon X had implanted fake memories into Wolverine's head, as well as into the heads of his teammates. And while Silver Fox and Wolverine did indeed live in their cabin, Silver Fox had not been killed that day. She survived to abandon Team X and become an agent of the criminal organization Hydra. Silver Fox finally reemerged in Wolverine's life when their former Team X colleague Mastodon was dying, but the former lovers' reunion was cut short when she was once again killed by Sabretooth in a familiar scene created by the powers of the reality-warping villain Psi-Borg. Wolverine then sadly returned to his cabin in the Canadian Rockies, burying Silver Fox's body for the second time.

SILVER FOX AS A HYDRA AGENT

Iron Fist #14

REAL NAME *Victor Creed*

OCCUPATION *Mercenary*

BASE *Mobile*

AFFILIATIONS *formerly X-Men, X-Factor, Brotherhood of Evil Mutants, Marauders, Team X*

POWERS/WEAPONS *Mutant healing factor, enhanced strength, senses, stamina, and speed. Retarded aging. Immune to most disease, poisons and toxins.*

Logan hated Victor Creed more than he hated anyone. Perhaps simply because they were so much alike.

After his mutant sharp teeth and claws first emerged when he was just a boy, Victor Creed was kept in a basement by his terrified parents.

SABRETOOTH

"Quod sum eris. I am what you will be."

ABILITY

Possessing the same basic powers as his rival Wolverine, Sabretooth had a few advantages over his longtime foe. He was seemingly older, had more experience, and lacked a conscience of any sort. He also worked willingly for Romulus, and therefore was privy to many of the shadowy manipulator's secrets.

BIRTHDAY SURPRISE

Although they had met in battle before, Logan gained his undying hatred for Creed in the Canadian Rocky Mountains when Sabretooth killed Logan's lover, a Native American named Silver Fox. Since this murder took place on Logan's birthday of all days, Sabretooth came up with the sick idea to plague Wolverine every year on that same date. On one such occasion, Creed endangered the life of another of Logan's girlfriends, Mariko Yashida.

LIFE STORY

Victor Creed probably wasn't born bad, but it was a close call. Although his background is shrouded in mystery due to the Weapon X program which altered and erased his memories, it is known that he suffered an abusive childhood. Victor's father thought his son was a devil spawn and routinely beat him, even once trying to remove his jagged teeth and claws with a set of pliers. Sabretooth somehow managed to escape his family's cruel persecution, and embarked on a life that would revisit the same brand of cruelty upon many that would cross his path.

Adopting the name Sabretooth, Creed first met Logan many years ago in Japan. Creed was about to add one more innocent victim to his count **(1)** when Logan interrupted him by cutting off Creed's hand. Sabretooth swore revenge, and soon ventured to Canada, to the same small mountain town that Logan had settled in with his lover, Silver Fox. Now taking orders from the lupine puppet master Romulus, Creed seemingly killed Silver Fox, and then beat Logan, throwing the young mutant in a deep pit, where he helped to brainwash him.

Both hailing from the same basic mutant family tree, Creed and Logan continued to see a lot of each other as the years went by. The two even found themselves on the same side of a fight for once as they both served on the Weapon X sponsored CIA strike force known as Team X **(2)**, with other mutant mercenaries such as the kinetic energy absorbing Maverick, the super-strong Mastodon, and Silver Fox, who had survived her encounter with Sabretooth in the cabin years ago—her original "death" perhaps a result of the fake memory implants that every member of Team X underwent from their Weapon X superiors. With their minds now altered into believing themselves friends, Logan and Creed fought on many missions together, traveling all over the world on behalf of the CIA, as well as for their secret employer, Romulus. It was during this time that Sabretooth had a liaison with the mutant shape-shifter Mystique, a romance that led to the birth of his son, Graydon Creed.

But of course Logan and Sabretooth's uneasy friendship couldn't last. When Sabretooth killed an innocent in order to teach Logan a lesson, Logan quit Team X, and the two's hatred was reinstated. Continuing his loyal service to Romulus, Sabretooth soon saw his feral enemy again when Logan was abducted by the Experiment X project. There, Creed savored a rare moment to torment his helpless foe.

When Logan escaped the clutches of the Canadian government and established himself as a Super Hero with the X-Men, Creed too upped the ante, and became a costume-clad Super Villain. Bouncing around from various teams and employers, Sabretooth fought Wolverine many times, as well as other heroes, including Iron Fist, Power Man, and Spider-Man **(3)**, and even the albino monster known as the Wendigo. Continuing in Romulus's service all the while, Creed's evil deeds finally caught up with him, when he finally pushed Logan past his limits after a battle in the labs of Experiment X **(4)**). In a conflict neither thought would truly ever happen, Wolverine won their final brawl **(5)**, killing Creed and avenging not just Silver Fox, but all the friends and lovers that Sabretooth had taken from him over the years.

"How long've we been dancing this dance Logan?... How many times have I left you for dead?"

WORLD WAR I

BRUTAL SUPERIOR

In 1912, a mere two years before the start of World War I, Logan trained with the Canadian military in a secret installation run by a mysterious man going by the name Hudson. A new recruit, Wolverine fell under the command of the sadistic Silas Burr.

Losing Janet

Hired by Hudson because of his unique ability to mold men into murderers and torturers, Burr was instructed to keep an eye on one soldier in particular: Logan. As Logan slowly fell in love with a fellow soldier named Janet, who was secretly under Hudson's employ as well, Burr soon received the order to murder her. It was Hudson's intent, or the intent of Romulus, the shadowy figure who had been manipulating Logan's life for years, to reduce the future Wolverine to nothing more than a killing machine. Logan would be forced to learn that if he ever strayed away from his brutal mission, if he ever attempted to reach out to someone, then that person would die. It was a lesson Logan had experienced before with his Native American lover Silver Fox, and it was one that he would be taught

Logan fought on behalf of Canada during World War I, growing more and more careless of his own safety as he was plunged into one bloody battle after another.

time and time again. On this particular occasion, Burr killed Janet, and then ripped out Logan's eye, driving the mutant into a frenzy. Romulus's control mechanism had worked. Logan retreated into the wild, until Sabretooth and Burr retrieved him. Logan's healing factor forced him to forget these traumatic memories and so made his mind a blank slate for Romulus to shape and control once again.

BLADES OF WAR

When battling the Germans in Belgium during World War I, Logan found himself in his element, a perfect soldier fighting for a noble cause. Brainwashed into forgetting that he had ever possessed bone claws, Logan broke off the bayonets from two rifles and stuck the jagged ends into his forearms when cornered by the enemy, instinctively creating makeshift claws for himself. Wolverine's refusal to quit on the field of battle would also aid him years later in 1937 when he found himself in the middle of the Spanish Civil War, fighting alongside none other than the writer Ernest Hemingway.

But in that 1915 fight in Belgium, the situation was much more dire than Logan would ever dream.

While busy defeating a small army of German soldiers, Logan was unaware that the field had been gassed by chlorine. He collapsed to the ground, and then seemingly recovered. However things weren't quite as they appeared, and after defeating the remaining soldiers, Logan noticed a strange man standing in the distance.

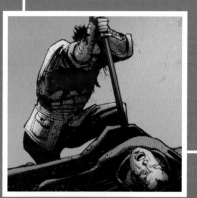

Death Stalks the Trenches

Without a word, the stranger and Logan began a duel, a fierce battle that ended with Logan plunging the stranger's sword through his chest. Thinking the battle was just another fight in a long life of conflict, Logan was unaware that he had just bested the Angel of Death himself, Lazaer, in a duel for his soul. Having emerged victorious, Logan returned to the land of the living and took to drinking heavily. He had defied the natural order of things, and his reward was a deep depression that he only fought off after being visited by Lazaer a second time.

MADRIPOOR

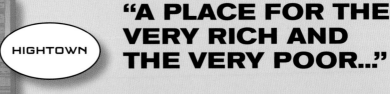

HIGHTOWN

LOWTOWN

"A PLACE FOR THE VERY RICH AND THE VERY POOR..."

It's a nation of polar opposites: From the ritzy spires of Hightown, to the ramshackle dwellings of Lowtown, one factor unites this small Asian country—crime.

SERAPH

Logan thought she was his saving grace, but in reality, she was his damnation. When Logan first met Seraph, the diminutive owner of Madripoor's Lowtown hangout the Princess Bar, the feral mutant was instantly attracted to the confident young woman. After a short fling Logan left Madripoor, but he renewed the relationship years later when he returned to the island. A brutal animal of a fighter, Logan was coached in the ways of subtlety and nuance by Seraph, as well as in the ways of love. He soon became her enforcer and killer, unaware that she too took her orders from a puppet master named Romulus.

"PATCH"

Years ago, when the public was under the impression that the X-Men had died, Wolverine decided to assume the identity of "Patch" when he made frequent visits to his home away from home— Madripoor. Since he had utilized this identity in the past, he seemed to blend in rather easily with the Asian island's residents, gaining a reputation there as one of the fabled co-owners of the Princess Bar.

Though his fellow X-Men have visited him on occasion in Madripoor, Logan would prefer that they stayed away from his private turf.

"Night's my kind'a time. An' this, my kind'a town."

History

An island nation located to the south of Singapore, Madripoor has a long history of criminal ties. Taken over by pirates centuries ago, the country has never been able to exorcise its delinquent demons. Instead it has embraced its corrupt history, developing a sort of laissez-faire government that turns a blind eye to criminal dealings, and, in fact, has a controlling interest in most of its major illegal activities. With the island offering sanctuary to any criminal inclined to visit its shores plus an extensive docking area and dozens of illegal airstrips, Madripoor's chief import is crime itself.

When Logan again began to frequent the island in the later years of his life, he realized that the country offered everything he needed in the way of an escape. Infested with the ninja clan the Hand, as well as thousands of other rough customers, Madripoor had just the clientele Logan was looking to rub elbows with, or trade punches with, when he needed a break from the moral highroad the X-Men always traveled.

As he became more and more settled into his home away from home, Logan even helped bring his friend (and sometimes lover) Tyger Tiger to power. By instating mob boss Tyger to such a position of power, Logan was able to keep tabs on the entire nation's underworld, and simultaneously end the country's drug trade. Wolverine also became close friends with Tai, the Chief of Police; Archie Corrigan, a loyal pilot; and Karma, the former New Mutant who was sucked into the corrupt world of her uncle, General Nguyen Ngoc Coy.

Years later, Logan would effectually change the entire landscape of the country yet again when he agreed to marry terrorist Viper in a ploy to help unite the citizens under her rule.

Logan battled the Silver Samurai for the mysterious black blade.

Employed by General Coy, Bloodscream and Roughouse fought "Patch" a number of times, and nearly always met defeat.

The RETURN

With all of his memories returned to him in the aftermath of the House of M event, Logan went back to Madripoor in order to visit the grave of his former lover Seraph, who had been killed by Sabretooth years earlier. Employing the help of his old friend Tai, Wolverine finally tracked down Seraph's gravesite, only after discovering that Tai, too, was a servant of Seraph's mysterious employers. Before giving away any more information to Wolverine, Tai quickly killed himself instead.

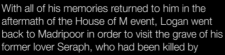

Never knowing the name of his life's mysterious manipulator, Wolverine finally discovered it, carved into the inside of Seraph's grave.

Notable current and former residents of Madripoor include:

Prince Baran, former ruler (deceased)

Archie Corrigan, owner of South Seas Skyways (deceased)

Crimelord General Nguyen Ngoc Coy (deceased)

Karma, member of the New Mutants and niece to General Nguyen Ngoc Coy

Tyger Tiger (Jessan Hoan), former revolutionary and current head of state

Tai, chief of police (deceased)

Jessica Drew, private investigator

Lindsay McCabe, actress

Viper, terrorist and recently deposed ruler of Madripoor

The idea of Mariko Yashida, heir to the powerful Yashida Clan, dating a *gaijin* such as Wolverine had upset many people. However, the young woman herself appeared undeterred until her father, Lord Shingen, returned after a mysterious absence and resumed leadership of his clan. Shingen forbade his daughter to date Logan, and forced her to marry the abusive Noburu-Hideki instead. So, Wolverine returned to Japan to set things right, launching a bloody crusade that saw him battle hundreds of ninjas from the criminal order known as the Hand, team up with the renegade martial artist thrill-seeker named Yukio, and expose Lord Shingen for the criminal he was. Wolverine won his love back, but Shingen and Noburu, were not quite so fortunate, and both died in the conflict.

Wolverine in

JAPAN

THE LAND OF THE RISING SUN HAS BEEN LOGAN'S HOME AS WELL AS HIS BATTLEGROUND.

KITTY PRYDE

When the young X-Man Kitty Pryde witnessed her father being intimidated by some Japanese businessmen, including the martial artist Ogun, she stowed away on a plane to Tokyo, to make sure her father wasn't harmed. On the run from the authorities with no money and no place to stay, Kitty fell into Ogun's murderous hands. Fortunately, she had previously alerted Wolverine. Ogun used telepathic techniques to grant Kitty a lifetime's worth of training in a few hours. The naïve mutant became his brainwashed pawn, and initially turned on Wolverine. Wolverine had trained with Ogun in his youth, before the sensei's fall from grace, and was not about to let him manipulate the young Miss Pryde. Wolverine stormed Ogun's dojo, killing his former instructor, and rescuing Kitty.

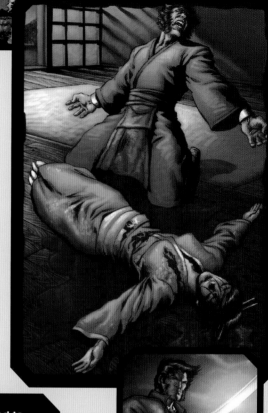

WOLVERINE'S AFFINITY WITH JAPAN

JASMINE FALLS

Logan returned to Japan in an attempt to find peace from his animalistic nature, as well as freedom from the programming forced onto him by the mysterious Romulus. Upon Ogun's suggestion, Logan traveled to Jasmine Falls to train with Bando Suboro. Before the training began, Suboro insisted that Logan should build his own house. Literally. So Logan did just that, building a house with his own two hands. He also took a beautiful villager named Itsu to be his wife. Itsu soon became pregnant, but her blissful life with Logan was about to come to an end. First Logan failed a test of battle, losing face with the village. Then he returned to his home to find Itsu lying dead, murdered by persons unknown.

Disillusioned, Logan traveled to the mountain home of Muramasa, allowing the corrupt ancient one to mold his anger into a blade that was even capable of killing Logan himself.

Perhaps his longest relationship to date, Wolverine's love affair with Japan has dated back decades.

Logan first journeyed to Japan sometime before World War II in order to train in the ways of Eastern philosophy and martial arts. Studying under the renowned martial artist Ogun, Logan revealed a knack for the controlled techniques, and was able to incorporate his love for bladed weaponry by mastering the art of the samurai's *katana* blade. Developing an appreciation for Japan's rich traditions and history, as well as a basic understanding of the language, Logan would later rely on this knowledge when escaping a Japanese prison camp during the latter stages of World War II.

Yukio

Amiko

Kenuichio Harada

Gom Kaishek

Haan Kaishek

Kia Kaishek

BLOOD DEBT

During a trip to Japan to visit his former lover Yukio and his near-daughter Amiko, Wolverine was taken by surprise when Kenuichio Harada, the Silver Samurai, appeared at Yukio's home, with hundreds of ninjas on his tail. It seems that Clan Yashida, now headed by Harada, was in the midst of a hostile takeover battle by rival brothers Gom and Haan Kaishek. Both brothers wanted to add the Yashida clan's organization to their crime portfolios, so they were waging a war against each other—a war that Logan fell directly into the center of when Gom kidnapped Yukio and Amiko. After fighting hordes of ninjas and criminals, Logan discovered the true devious mind behind the Kaishek family: Gom and Haan's power-hungry sister Kia. She had been playing each side against the other. With his true enemy now firmly in his sights, Logan rescued Yukio and defeated Kia in a brutal battle, ending the threat of the Kaishek clan for good.

TALK TO THE HAND

They emerge from the shadows unnoticed. Without a sound, and with a precision only obtained by a lifetime of martial arts training, they strike, with only the highest skilled prey even sensing the oncoming attack. They are the ancient and elite ninja clan known only as the Hand, and they've been a constant thorn in Wolverine's side ever since he first ventured to Japan.

When a boy named Kagenobu saved his mother by killing an attacker back in feudal Japan, his mother was imprisoned for his crime. With only his mother's bloody handprint on his shirt left to remember her by, the boy grew into a man, and founded the Hand, a ninja order without equal.

Distinguished by their long-established ties to the mystical and arcane, the Hand's members have frequently participated in a resurrection ritual in which several members sacrifice their lives in order to raise a person from the dead. Likewise, when a member of the Hand is killed in battle, he disappears into a puff of smoke and ash, his duties fulfilled to his clan.

A criminal organization whose deadly services are often available to the highest bidder, the Hand has been opposed by a variety of heroes, including Wolverine, Daredevil, and Elektra, the latter of whom was actually a member of the evil organization for a good part of her life. Wolverine in particular has no love lost for this clan of assassins, and no qualms about dispatching hundreds of their number in his customary deadly fashion.

VAUGHAN • RISSO • WHITE
issue number two of three

Publication date
May 2008

Editor-in-chief
Joe Quesada

Cover artist
Eduardo Risso

Writer
Brian K. Vaughan

Penciller
Eduardo Risso

Inker
Eduardo Risso

Colorist
Dean White

Letterer
Joe Caramagna

Wolverine:
LOGAN
miniseries
#2

"**Folks don't die like they used to... these days, nobody remembers how to stay in their plots.**" WOLVERINE

MAIN CHARACTERS: Wolverine, Ethan Warren, Atsuko
LOCATION: Hiroshima, Japan

Background

Brian K. Vaughan had become a comics superstar. With his hit Vertigo comic series *Y: The Last Man*, his Marvel cult favorite *Runaways*, and his contributions to the popular ABC television show *Lost* added to his resumé, Vaughan had begun to take on more projects, each a success in its own right. Deciding to return to Marvel to write a few limited series, Vaughan penned a *Dr. Strange* mini, as well as the three-issue *Logan* series, a comic that leapt from the past to the present and back again, detailing one of Wolverine's last World War II adventures.

However, Vaughan wasn't alone in his effort. He was joined on the title by artist Eduardo Risso, another comics luminary with a large fan base. Risso had made a name for himself drawing the critical *noir* smash *100 Bullets* with acclaimed writer Brian Azzarello over at Vertigo, and had also partnered with that same co-creator for a limited *Batman* arc. With Risso's considerable storytelling talents on board, Logan was a surefire hit for the duo, Wolverine's eager fans devouring the series's well-crafted insights into their favorite hero's enigmatic past.

The Story

Wolverine returns to Hiroshima to reminisce about a past love and battle an old enemy who has been reduced to a mutated ghost of his former self...

1

2

3

4

5

6

7

Logan was on a journey to his past. Needless to say, the trip wouldn't be a pleasant one. With his memories returned to him in the aftermath of the House of M event, Logan traveled to Hiroshima, Japan, in order to settle a long-standing score. There, he was attacked by a flaming figure from the shadows, a mutated burning skeleton, more dead than alive **(1)**. And while the two battled, the man's scent caught Logan's attention, and brought a flood of memories rushing back.

Logan's thoughts returned to the last days of World War II. Captured by the Japanese, Logan was thrown into a cell at their POW camp, along with an American soldier named Ethan Warren. After utilizing his mutant powers to escape, Logan and Warren found themselves at a crossroads where they encountered a Japanese woman named Atsuko. To cover their trail, Warren wanted to shoot the innocent woman with the rifles they'd stolen from their Japanese captors. Logan wouldn't allow this and insisted that he and Warren part ways, a request made at gunpoint. Warren reluctantly retreated into the surrounding forest, leaving Logan alone with the grateful Atsuko.

Taking her savior to her home to hide him for the night, Atsuko and Logan soon found that conversation quickly turned to romance **(2)**. The next morning, their love affair was brutally cut short by a thunderous gunshot **(3)**. As Logan fell to the ground next to Atsuko, Ethan Warren appeared in the doorway, loaded rifle still in hand **(4)**. Warren approached Atsuko, and the young woman, anger replacing her fear, charged the American soldier, attacking him with her dead father's samurai sword. The two fought viciously. Atsuko was skilled in martial arts, but Warren's brute strength and ruthlessness won out. He ran her through with his bayonet and the young woman fell to the ground dead **(5)**.

But Ethan Warren didn't know much about the man he thought he had murdered. Revelling in his triumph over Atsuko, Warren was caught unaware as Logan pounced, his mutant healing factor having mended his gunshot wound. As their fight continued out into the open countryside, Logan discovered that he and Ethan were more alike than he ever could have suspected. Ethan was also a mutant. He could be injured, but not killed **(6)**.

The sudden sound of an aircraft—a US bomber—flying overhead caused Logan and Warren to break off from their bloody battle. As they looked on, the plane dropped a single bomb. The nuclear device exploded, devastating the city of Hiroshima **(7)**. A lone figure emerged from the smoking ruins—the mutilated and charred form of Logan **(8)**.

The *Logan* miniseries concluded in the following issue. The scene switched back to the present. Locked in a battle with the burning remains of the man who used to be Ethan Warren, Logan was seemingly defeated when Warren ripped out his heart. After eating the organ, Warren's body was made whole and solid again, his appearance only making Logan more enraged and determined to destroy his foe. Lunging forward and leading with his claws, Logan managed to behead Warren, collapsing to the ground next to him only after he was sure of his enemy's demise. Awaking from a vivid dream in which he bid a final farewell to Atsuko, Logan rose to his feet just in time to watch the sunrise break through the nearby trees.

"ALL I REMEMBER IS A TEARDROP FALLING FROM THE SKY."

8

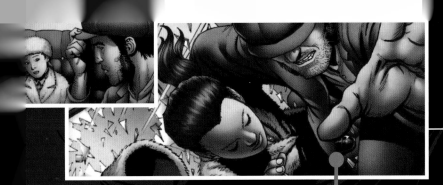

Logan first met Natalia Romanova, the future Black Widow, when he was traveling to meet her father, the infamous Russian spy, Taras Romanova. In order to make sure Logan wasn't followed, Taras had the mutant's train hijacked.

With his mind once again wiped by the evil Romulus's manipulations, Logan trained with Taras for two years, learning about the information trade, before following his orders and killing his new mentor. Meanwhile, Logan was training Natalia as well, trying to get her to escape this cruel life.

"I wanted her to have a fightin' chance—which meant teachin' her how to fight. An' fight dirty."

BLACK WIDOW

To her, Logan will always be her "Little Uncle." This was the name super-spy Black Widow gave the hero after he first saved her life. Widow's childhood protector has since become her trusted ally.

Logan was reunited with his prize student years later, when he rescued her from the clutches of Baron Von Strucker, with a little help from another legendary hero, Captain America.

On a mission for SHIELD, Black Widow was ambushed by the Hand. Wolverine helped fight off her attackers, and then partnered with his old protégée to take the fight to the ninjas themselves.

FIRST APPEARANCE
Tales of Suspense #52

REAL NAME *Natalia (Natasha) Romanova*

OCCUPATION *Government operative as part of the Initiative program*

BASE *New York City*

AFFILIATIONS *Avengers, SHIELD, Champions, Lady Liberators, KGB*

POWERS/WEAPONS *Age retardation due to Super Hero serum. Bracelets contain "widow's line" and "widow's bite" electronic charge. Suction cups in boots and gloves allow adhesion to most surfaces. Plastic explosives in belt. Expert martial artist and gymnast.*

OTHER ADVENTURES
Before Black Widow became a Super Hero and later joined the Avengers, she and Logan met several times as espionage agents. On one occasion, Black Widow saved Logan and Nick Fury from a car-full of Hydra agents. On another, the two found themselves on opposite sides when Ben Grimm and Logan invaded Russian airspace.

WORLD WAR II

His life was already a battlefield. The war only made it official. With his secret ops activities supposedly aiding his native Canada in the conflict, Logan saw nothing but action during World War II. Serving with various battalions or performing covert operations for his employers, Logan's experiences on the front line ranged in location from Japan to the Italian Alps, Poland to Normandy.

MADRIPOOR

In 1941, on the small Asian island of Madripoor, Logan jumped into a fight against the ninja clan known as the Hand, not really caring who it was that the Hand was ganging up on. Any excuse to tackle this outlaw band of killers and assassins was good enough for Logan, despite the overwhelming odds. When the dust finally cleared, and the bodies of the dead Hand began to dissolve into the night air, Wolverine first met the man whose life he'd saved, the hero known as Captain America.

THE DEVIL'S BRIGADE

Under the sadistic command of Silas Burr, the man who would later become the Super Villain known as Cyber, Logan served in the Devil's Brigade. This team of cutthroat soldiers fought for Canada, although several of them, including Logan, took orders from a secret organization. Logan's orders came from his contact in Madripoor, a woman named Seraph who owned his favorite dive, the Princess Bar. And Seraph's orders came from the mysterious Romulus, a man who seemed to never tire of manipulating the events of Logan's life, as well as his very thoughts and memories. It was Romulus who ordered Logan to take part in Operation: Blueboy, a mission that saw Logan once again partnering with the American hero, Captain America. Teaming with Cap, and Cap's partner Bucky, Logan set out to take down Baron Von Strucker, one of Hitler's right-hand men.

"AN' JUST LIKE IN THE FIRST WORLD WAR, WE DID THE DEVIL'S WORK."

FURY

To meet up with Captain America, Logan was first introduced to his liaison, an American by the name of Sergeant Nick Fury. Logan quickly learned that Fury was a master tactician, devising ingenious attack plans at a moment's notice. Together, the two saved Captain America and his troops from a small army of attackers. But soon it was Fury's turn to be impressed as the group closed in on Von Strucker. In fact, Fury was so impressed by his brothers in arms that when, years later, he became the head of a world peacekeeping force, he named it SHIELD, after Cap's own weapon of choice.

POLAND

Of all the horrors Logan faced during the war, none matched the terrible cruelty displayed in the Sobibor concentration camp in Poland. The head of this Nazi death camp had recently committed suicide and his replacement, Major Bauman, was determined to make a name for himself among his superiors. Ruthlessly ambitious, Bauman resolved to increase the camp's productivity and kill rate. Almost immediately, however, the Major's plans encountered a roadblock. A short and silent roadblock going by the name Prisoner Zero. A prisoner known in certain other parts of the world as Logan.

When this stubborn prisoner refused to work, Bauman ordered him to be shot, an execution the Nazi personally witnessed. So it came as quite a surprise to the Major when, the following night, he saw the very same prisoner standing about as if nothing had happened. As the Major tried time and time again to kill this seemingly unkillable man, he slowly lost his grip on sanity, and died in a fire of his own making, aware, in his final moments, of the truth of his situation. Prisoner Zero wasn't trapped in the camp with him. He was trapped in the camp with Prisoner Zero.

JAPAN

In the closing days of World War II, Logan awoke in a POW camp outside of Hiroshima, Japan. Alongside an American named Lieutenant Ethan Warren, Logan devised a plan to escape, one involving brute force and the element of surprise. On the run from their guards in the Japanese wilderness, Logan and Ethan came to an irreconcilable impasse when they stumbled upon a Japanese civilian woman named Atsuko. Logan wished to spare the innocent woman's life, while Ethan wished to kill her to cover his tracks. However, the dispute would end in violence, as Logan and his companion were soon caught in the explosion of a nuclear bomb dropped by the Americans.

Logan received his first taste of Captain America's amazing leadership abilities when the two teamed up during World War II in order to take down Baron Von Strucker. Logan's respect for Cap deepened when the two fought side by side in Djerba.

"My orders were to stick close to Captain America an' see what I could find out about him—but there was more I wanted to know."

Captain America and Logan were both under strict orders during World War II. Cap was to win a minor skirmish and thereby establish himself as a hero in his fellow troops' eyes. Logan was to shadow Cap, and then kill him. Captain America's orders came from the American military itself. Wolverine's orders came from a mysterious covert entity called Romulus. But when both heroes discovered that the evil Baron Von Strucker was involved, they changed their plans, not wanting to let this former Nazi form his own terrorist group, which came to be called Hydra.

Captain America, his sidekick Bucky, and Logan stormed Strucker's stronghold and managed to take the villain hostage. However, on their way home, their plane was shot out of the sky by the evil Baron Zemo. Everything was going according to Romulus's plan. Logan was now supposed to subdue Cap and hand him over to the war criminal Baron Zemo. But Logan had his own ideas.

Despite being brainwashed by Romulus, Logan could see the error of his ways. So when he fought Cap, he intentionally took a beating, giving Captain America and Bucky a chance to rally. Zemo and Strucker fled, and Logan was knocked unconscious, Captain America never realizing the mutant's brave sacrifice.

Logan and Captain America's sidekick Bucky never saw eye to eye, perhaps because their personalities were too much alike.

THE WINTER SOLDIER

Even though he spent the majority of his life perceived as a punch line, Bucky Barnes didn't have a humorous bone in his entire body. Placed by the US military as Captain America's right-hand man, Bucky was, in fact, an agent of Romulus, following the secret agenda of this mysterious master manipulator. Despite appearances, Bucky was a creature of wild fury, like Logan, a cold-blooded killer sent to keep tabs on Captain America, the US's number one hero. After his supposed death during the closing days of World War II and his return as the Winter Soldier, Bucky's orders would lead him once again into conflict with Logan when he was ordered by Romulus to murder Logan's first wife, Itsu, in order to drive Logan into a mad frenzy.

UNLIKELY PARTNERS

As World War II drew to a close, Captain America went down in a plane crash, his body frozen solid in ice on the ocean's floor. He was revived by the Avengers decades later and once again renewed his career as a Super Hero. Meanwhile, Wolverine finally broke the grip of Romulus's evil manipulations, and was no longer brainwashed by his shadowy forces. Wolverine took up residence with the X-Men, and began to enjoy Super Hero status himself. With such similar professions, it was no surprise that Captain America and Wolverine would wind up side by side on the field of battle many times in the years to come.

On one memorable occasion, Wolverine came across a giant robot after a night at a local New York pub. By chance or by fate, Captain America was tracking the same mechanical monster. The two heroes combined their efforts to battle the adamantium-covered robot, which was named Tess, and its mutant master, the villainous Overrider. Wolverine and Cap managed to defeat the robot by severing its head, an act achieved by Cap literally hammering Wolverine's claws into the automaton's neck.

FIRST APPEARANCE
Captain America Comics #1

REAL NAME *Steven Rogers*

OCCUPATION *Adventurer*

BASE *formerly Avengers Tower*

AFFILIATIONS *Avengers, Invaders, Redeemers*

POWERS/WEAPONS *Peak physical condition and endurance granted by super-soldier serum. Expert martial artist and boxer. Superb tactician. Near indestructible vibranium shield.*

"PAL... I GOT NO TIME FOR YOUR SELF-RIGHTEOUS BULL!"

Wolverine to Captain America

FURTHER ADVENTURES

As Super Heroes are prone to do in times of global crisis, when events require super-teams and individual heroes to join together against a common enemy, Wolverine and Captain America have often fought side by side. Logan and Cap battled together when taking on the Beyonder on his futuristic Battleworld in the Secret Wars. They joined forces to help thwart the mad god Thanos when he tried to lay claim to the mystical Infinity Gauntlet and likewise on all of creation itself. And they became teammates as they took on a renegade faction of the government agency SHIELD, despite Cap's initial misgivings. With common enemies like Hydra and Magneto, Cap and Logan partnered more times than either would like to admit, until Cap's untimely death at the hands of his bitter foe the Red Skull.

SHIELD

NICK FURY
Founder of SHIELD and its longest-serving Director to date, Nick Fury has spent his lifetime in action, easily adapting from war hero to super spy and keeper of the global peace.

It could be said that Wolverine was a part of SHIELD even before the organization began. Its title originally standing for Supreme Headquarters International Espionage Law-Enforcement Division and then later the Strategic Hazard Intervention Espionage Logistics Directorate, the world peacekeeping agency has had a file on Wolverine since its inception. Which is not at all surprising, as Logan has known the organization's founder, Nick Fury, since their days together in World War II.

The pair first met during Operation: Blueboy, a secret mission involving Captain America. Logan observed Fury's brilliant strategic mind at work while Fury learned exactly how efficient a fighter Logan was and later employed him as a freelance espionage agent. On one important mission, Fury teamed Logan with adventurers Carol Danvers and Ben Grimm on a mission to steal Russian secrets.

After becoming SHIELD's director, Fury continued to ask Logan for help on the occasional mission, including what would become Fury's final mission with the super spy organization. During his so-called Secret War, Fury crossed a line resulting in a conflict in the heart of Manhattan, and was not only removed from his Director's seat, but reduced to being a fugitive from the law.

IRON MAN
After Nick Fury was fired from his position as Director, SHIELD promoted agent Maria Hill to the role. Her tenure at the helm would be short-lived however, as she soon stepped down to make way for Tony Stark, aka Iron Man.

ENEMY OF THE STATE

When Wolverine was brainwashed by the Hand into doing their bidding, SHIELD freed him from his programming. Afterward, Wolverine and the ninja assassin Elektra teamed up with SHIELD's task force to take down both the Hand, and the terrorist cell known as Hydra.

Acting on the orders of special agent Timothy "Dum Dum" Dugan, Wolverine and Elektra prepared to storm Hydra's base and do battle with the Gorgon—the man who had put Wolverine under the Hand's deadly spell in the first place.

HYDRA

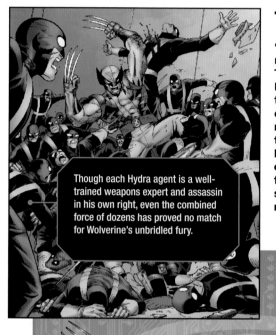

Though each Hydra agent is a well-trained weapons expert and assassin in his own right, even the combined force of dozens has proved no match for Wolverine's unbridled fury.

THE HORDES

"Cut off a limb, and two more shall take its place." The motto of the agents of Hydra reveals much about their unwavering dedication. Like its ancient namesake of Greek myth, the organization known as Hydra has proven extremely hard to kill, as its followers often willingly sacrifice their lives for their maniacal cause.

BARON VON STRUCKER
A former ally of Nazi leader Adolf Hitler and Captain America's arch foe the Red Skull, Baron Wolfgang von Strucker founded Hydra during World War II, and later became known as the organization's Supreme Hydra.

A subversive institution with a goal of nothing less than world domination, Hydra sprang out of World War II as a grab for power by Nazi Baron von Strucker. As his organization grew into its own kind of dangerous animal, SHIELD was born to combat it, created from an initial idea of Strucker's greatest wartime foe, Nick Fury. After the first Director of SHIELD was assassinated by a Hydra effort, Fury was promoted to replace him, perfectly positioned to continue his war against his longtime enemy.

Wolverine's close relationship with SHIELD during much of his adult life has afforded him much experience of dealing with Hydra. During the World War II effort dubbed Operation: Blueboy, Logan helped Nick Fury and Captain America overthrow a Hydra uprising. Years later, during his freelance espionage days, Logan was ambushed by Hydra troops while trying to research his adamantium skeleton. On that occasion, he was saved by two CIA agents, none other than the future Ms. Marvel, Carol Danvers, and Nick Fury himself. Today, Hydra continues to rear its many ugly heads in Wolverine's world, the organization even trying to manipulate Logan's teammate and friend Spider-Woman into betraying her New Avengers team.

When Logan was brainwashed by the Hand, he also became Hydra's premier agent, as the evil institutions were working in tandem at the time. Forced to do everything from invading the headquarters of the Fantastic Four, to attacking the blind Super Hero Daredevil in his own home, and battling local cops on the street, Wolverine was Hydra's violent lap dog until he was apprehended by SHIELD.

MADAME HYDRA
Also known as Viper, Madame Hydra has had a long connection to the criminal organization whose name she shares, as well as a long history with Wolverine himself. At one point, the two were even married when Viper blackmailed Logan. However, Wolverine was soon able to turn the tables on his "wife" and demand a divorce.

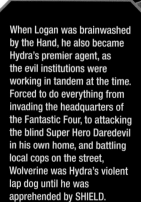

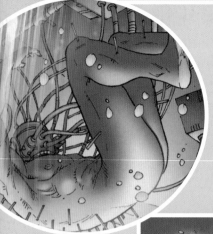

DEATH OF A SPY

Logan's memories had always been spotty at best. Although his mutant healing factor saved his life more times than he could remember, it also helped heal his damaged psyche, erasing painful memories from his mind. So, when Logan first recalled his work for Team X, a CIA strike force funded by the government's secret Weapon X division, he remembered Janice Hollenbeck as his lover and as a communist double agent, caught in the wrong place at the wrong time.

When Logan later recovered all of his lost memories, he realized Janice wasn't his lover, but merely a tragic acquaintance.

Sabretooth had in fact killed Janice just to make a point to Logan, his CIA teammate. The team had been supposed to rescue Janice and sabotage the Soviets' Omega Red project.

Wolverine's Cold War

FALSE MEMORIES

His hazy past made him the perfect test subject. When Logan began work for Team X, his mind was altered even further as the Weapon X program implanted him with false memories, the better to control him. With his mind a clean slate, Weapon X programmers were able to team Logan with his old enemy Sabretooth, and even his former love Silver Fox, without Logan remembering a shred of their history together. Other Team X members included strongman Mastodon and fellow mutant Maverick.

When Logan later recalled his time with Team X, he realized that, years ago in the Canadian Rockies, Silver Fox had survived Sabretooth's murderous attack after all.

STRANGE MEETING
Logan has spent much of his long life working for clandestine organizations of one kind or another. For a while he was a freelance operative for the interdimensional firm of Landau, Luckman and Lake. He began running missions for this improbable company after meeting a man named Chang shortly after World War I. Logan's adventures began to take a fantastic turn, as he found himself traveling to strange new worlds.

By appealing to Logan's sense of duty, Chang talked his old friend back into the espionage game while Logan was living in Jasmine Falls.

Chasing after a man named Kimora, Logan journeyed into another dimension in order to settle an old score.

Before defeating the world-conquering Kimora, Logan first had to best his soldiers, some of whom could seemingly control the shadows themselves.

Throughout his life, Logan has been a soldier fighting other men's wars, working as a CIA agent as well as for the enigmatic Romulus.

Known only by a single name, Logan became a favorite operative of both America's and Canada's secret services.

NUKE
In 1953, Logan once again fell under the control of his shadowy manipulator, the callous man known only as Romulus. Working as one of his ruthless operatives, Logan helped participate in turning a boy named Frank Simpson into the deranged super-soldier Nuke. Growing up watching his alcoholic mother verbally abuse his meek father, young Frank was influenced by his babysitter, also an operative of Romulus's, into killing his mother.

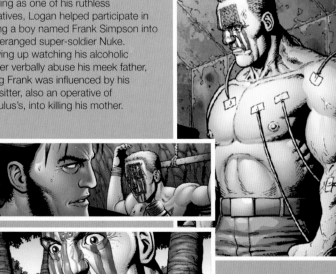

Logan later met Frank during the Vietnam War. He tortured the already unstable soldier, carving the Stars and Stripes onto the man's face, and pushed him over the edge.

YEARS LATER, WOLVERINE AND NUKE FACED OFF IN A FINAL CONFRONTATION IN THE FIELDS OF VIETNAM

WEAPON X

1

2

3

1 PROFESSOR
ANDRÉ THORTON

2 DR. ABRAHAM
CORNELIUS

3 CAROL HINES

A STORM WAS COMING. Logan could feel it. The sins of his past were finally catching up with the feral mutant, and he had begun to drink heavily in a futile attempt to chase them away. After accidentally injuring a fellow operative at a gun range, Logan was ordered to take a leave of absence from his intelligence work for the Canadian government. This demotion only furthered his descent into depression. Living in a cheap motel, plagued with terrifying nightmares, Logan decided to take a trip up to the Yukon, hoping to escape whatever fateful tempest was brewing. One night, as he exited a bar, Logan was jumped by three armed men. After a hopeless struggle, he awoke in the chambers of Canada's secret Department K, the test subject for what would become known as Experiment X.

Logan was poked and prodded, and then hooked up to an elaborate life-support system. Adamantium was fed into his body, the unbreakable metal merging with the bones of his skeleton.

As a group of scientists including Dr. Abraham Cornelius and Carol Hines looked on, the man in charge of Department K, the mysterious Professor André Thorton, quickly left the test chamber. Unaware that his test subject was a mutant with a healing factor, the professor was astonished that Logan could survive the agonizing process. In fact, despite the air he would maintain around his coworkers, the Professor was just like every other employee at Experiment X, a puppet being manipulated by a mastermind lurking in the wings. A mastermind that Logan would learn, years later, was his lifelong enemy, Romulus.

"Mr. Logan..."

Though Logan put up a valiant struggle, his three attackers had the numbers, the stun gun, and the element of surprise.

PHUP!

THE PROCESS
The hair on his body shaved, Logan was placed, unconscious, in a tank of special ingredients and nutrients. His body was punctured by hundreds of needles, wires, and tubes, which allowed adamantium to infuse with his skeleton. Owing to his healing factor, Logan survived the transfusion, to the surprise of all in attendance. He was now deemed ready for the next stage. However, Logan had other revelations in store for his capturers: revelations that emerged in triplicate from the backs of his hands.

"HE'S GOT LIKE... SPIKES COMING OUT OF HIM!"

"MAGNIFICENT..."

THE CLAWS APPEAR As his now adamantium-covered claws shot from the back of his hands, Logan regained consciousness. In a fit of uncontrollable rage, he began to wreak havoc in the laboratory. His mind was so disturbed that he killed a lab technician. Professor Thorton could not have been happier. He had found his perfect killing machine. He had found Weapon X.

THE ANIMAL

Logan was not proving to be the ideal test subject after all. Reduced to a feral state due to the adamantium bonding process, the man who would become Wolverine made every attempt to escape his bonds. Despite his constant struggles, the Department K staff remained one step ahead of him. Thanks to the expertise of Dr. Abraham Cornelius, Logan's mind was tampered with, allowing the Weapon X staff to literally probe his thoughts and see into his mind on their monitors.

BREAKOUT

GASSED

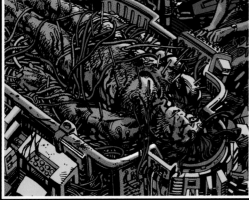

CONFINED

"WHAT'S THE POINT OF THIS WEAPON IF WE CAN'T CONTROL HIM?"

ESCAPE

As the staff at Department K continued to make progress on their Weapon X program, they began to run field tests on Logan, releasing him into the wild in order to pit his abilities against wolves and bears **(1)**. The mutant was fitted with a futuristic helmet and a battery pack of sorts, which enabled Dr. Cornelius and the other handlers to control his every movement. Logan was nothing more than a remote-controlled toy **(2)**. They even made Logan slaughter the citizens of an entire town called Roanoke, in order to test their killing machine's efficiency.

Finally, Logan's amazing willpower and berserker strength overpowered the tranquilizers in his system. With unbridled fury, Logan tore his way through the Department K installation, killing dozens of hired soldiers and staff members. As Professor Thorton, Dr. Cornelius, and Carol Hines gathered in a control room, hoping and praying to stay alive, Logan burst in and ran Cornelius through with his claws. Even as the Professor set the mutant's body on fire in a fission chamber in a last ditch effort to destroy him, Logan toughed through the pain, and thrust his claws deep into the Professor's skull **(3)**.

However, as is usually the case with the Weapon X program, not everything was as it seemed. Logan had not freed himself and murdered his tormentors. The whole scenario was merely a fantasy that had played out on Dr. Cornelius's monitor. It was all just the fondest desire of the caged beast, broadcast for the entertainment and enlightenment of the Experiment X staff.

Nevertheless, Department K had tempted fate. This fictional taste of freedom was all Logan needed in the way of inspiration. Soon, he had actually freed himself from his bonds and escaped into the night **(4)**.

1

2

3

4

INTO THE WILD

For whatever reason, Logan did not kill his tormentors that night. Because of his mercy, Dr. Cornelius, Carol Hines, and Professor Thorton would all return to plague him in later years. However, Logan did not display the same amount of compassion for those foolish enough to get in his way during his escape. Still more animal than man, the mutant tore a bloody path through guard after guard, until he was finally free to vanish into the snow-covered Canadian wilderness. And as a blizzard raged around his slow procession into the woods, perhaps some little part of his mind made a note of the storm he had just survived.

THE HISTORY OF WEAPON X

The roots of the Experiment X program date back to World War II, when Professor Thorton discovered an experimental lab beneath a liberated concentration camp once belonging to the future X-Men antagonist calling himself Mr. Sinister. Using the evil mutant's experiments as a basis for his own technology, Thorton hatched the Weapons Plus program with the blessing of the US government. Later, the program would become a joint effort with Canada's clandestine Department K government division.

The project began by adopting the technology of the US government's Operation: Rebirth experiment. This led to the creation of the war hero Captain America, and was thereafter referred to as Weapon I. The second two projects were animal experiments, and Weapons IV, V, and VI were performed on various ethnic minorities. By the next three test subjects, Weapons VII through IX, the decision was made to use superhuman test subjects. Logan was the finest known specimen to date and the Professor was ordered to

abduct him to become Weapon X.

Despite their failure to control the man who would become Wolverine, the Weapon Plus program continued operations, its various experiments resulting in the creation of several future superhuman players, such as the mysterious Fantomex, the mercenary Deadpool, the wild Native, and the secret agent Maverick, who later changed his name to Agent Zero.

AGENT ZERO

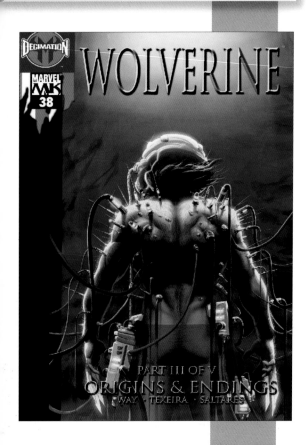

Publication date
March 2006

Editor-in-chief
Joe Quesada

Cover Artist
Kaare Andrews

Writer
Daniel Way

Breakdowns
Javier Saltares

Finishes
Mark Texeira

Colorist
J. D. Smith

Letterer
Randy Gentile

WOLVERINE #38

"I hate the memories. For so long, I wanted 'em back... An' it's like the saying goes: 'be careful what you wish for.' !"

WOLVERINE

MAIN CHARACTERS: Wolverine, Muramasa, Winter Soldier
SUPPORTING CHARACTERS: Muramasa's samurai, deceased Weapon X employees, Iron Man, Captain America
LOCATIONS: Department K, Canada; Jasmine Falls, Japan; presumably New York City

Background

Marvel was finally ready to lay all its cards on the table, but they weren't about to do it quickly. After the success of the highly acclaimed miniseries *Origin*, Editor-in-Chief Joe Quesada felt confident that his audience was ready to have all the blanks filled in with regard to Wolverine's mysterious past. But since Logan had been the subject of so many memory implants and brainwashings in the course of his long lifespan, sorting out Wolverine's intricate history would be no simple task.

The first step was the *House of M* miniseries. In this epic tale, Logan was finally granted access to the entire catalog of his personal memories through the tampering of the reality-altering former hero, the Scarlet Witch. The next step was to create a forum for Logan to deal with these new memories. And so writer Daniel Way was commissioned to pen an arc of the regular *Wolverine* series that would help launch a companion title called *Wolverine: Origins*. Way began to weave a complex tapestry that set Logan on a journey back into his past, and straight into the heart of Weapon X.

The Story

Wolverine heads back to the now deserted Weapon X complex to learn if he truly had help when he escaped its clutches all those years ago...

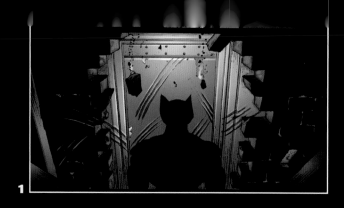

Wolverine now remembered everything. So for many government officials, it was finally time to panic. During the event referred to as the House of M, the former Avenger named the Scarlet Witch had inadvertently restored to Wolverine all his former memories. In doing so, she had shown Wolverine a side of himself, and a side of the world in general, that he realized he may have been better off not knowing. Pandora's demons could not be forced back into their box, so now Wolverine was left with a long list of debts—debts that he was determined to collect.

The first one on his list led him to visit his old rival the Silver Samurai in Tokyo, Japan. Logan severed the Samurai's hand with his claws, then interrogated his foe, discovering that the answers that he sought lay in Canada, at the clandestine Department K, the home of the Weapon X project. After stowing away on a freighter, Logan arrived at the door of his least favorite place on the planet **(1)**. Cutting his way into the facility, Logan discovered a secret doorway leading to a dark staircase and the true laboratories of Experiment X. Though he had returned to Weapon X several times before, on this particular occasion, Logan was armed with a full arsenal of his own memories, nightmares that haunted his every step. He remembered his rage when he escaped **(2)**, and the pain and overwhelming guilt that permeated his being. And despite having seen thousands of horrors and atrocities in his long life, Wolverine couldn't help but be appalled when he saw the scene he'd left behind: a roomful of rotting corpses, all murdered by his hand when he escaped the project years ago **(3)**.

As he reflected on the time the Weapon X program shaped him into a living weapon, he remembered the other period in his life when someone had concentrated his innate rage and feelings of hate into a tangible object. It was years ago in Jasmine Falls, after his wife Itsu had been killed by the order of Romulus, and by the bullet of the Winter Soldier. Logan had sought a focus for his anger, and had climbed a nearby mountain to meet the ancient Muramasa. Muramasa promised to distill Logan's pure, wild hatred into a fine blade, a sword capable of killing even Logan himself. However, after the mystic process was complete, Muramasa did not hand over the sword but commanded his samurai to dispose of the drained mutant **(4)**. As the samurai carried Logan through the thick forest **(5)**, the Winter Soldier shot and killed the samurai **(6)**, **(7)**, apprehended Logan, and took him to Madripoor, as he had been ordered.

Back in the present, Wolverine had seen enough. Discovering a bullet hole in the skull of one of the dead Weapon X technicians, Logan realized that the Silver Samurai had told him the truth. So he placed a call to Captain America **(8)**. He needed to speak to the man from his past who had rescued him from Weapon X, and if there was one person who would know his whereabouts, it was Cap. After all, who better than the former mentor of Bucky Barnes to help him locate the Winter Soldier **(9)**.

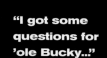

"I got some questions for 'ole Bucky..."

ADAMANTIUM 101

When was it discovered?

The virtually unbreakable metal adamantium is a complex steel alloy, the product of years of scientific research. As with many groundbreaking innovations, adamantium was created partly by accident.

During World War II, American scientist Dr. Myron MacLain stumbled onto the compound known as vibranium, a kind of indestructible steel. After molding the metal into a shield for the government's new super-soldier, Captain America, MacLain spent decades trying to reproduce the process. In the 1960s, instead of vibranium, he discovered that he had created adamantium.

Originally, the US government used adamantium for clandestine operations, and shared its formula with only a few trusted allies. Eventually, the metal fell into the wrong hands, and adamantium was introduced to the world at large when the Avengers' android villain Ultron showed up to a battle coated in the alloy.

DR. MYRON MACLAIN

EVEN THOR'S HAMMER HAS NO EFFECT

OMEGA RED

Are there different kinds?

TRUE ADAMANTIUM
Taking its name from the fabled metal adamantine in Greek mythology, adamantium is an extremely difficult and expensive alloy to produce. Its true composition a government secret, the metal is created by mixing several different resins. For eight minutes after the ingredients are mixed, the alloy can be molded and shaped if kept at 1,500° Fahrenheit, after which it cannot be altered by conventional means.

ADAMANTIUM BETA
When adamantium was bonded to Wolverine's bones, his healing factor altered its molecules to form a new variant, adamantium beta. This new variant allows the biological processes of the bones to continue as normal.

CARBONADIUM
Always wanting to keep up with American technology, the Soviet Union created carbonadium in an attempt to replicate the adamantium process. Though an extremely hard substance, carbonadium is much more malleable than the alloy it was based on, and is also highly radioactive, poisoning those unfortunate enough to come into close contact with it. In fact, carbonadium is so deadly it actually nullifies the mutant healing factor inherent to Wolverine and his ilk. After using the metal to augment the super-soldier Omega Red, Russian scientists are today still attempting to perfect its formula.

THE ALLOTROPES
There are several other metals that can be considered to fall into the adamantium family, including the metal's original predecessor vibranium, as well as its cousin, the anti-metal substance Antarctic vibranium.

How strong is it?

SECONDARY ADAMANTIUM
Due to the expensive nature of true adamantium, oftentimes certain parties will opt to manufacture secondary adamantium instead. This material is much stronger than titanium. Secondary adamantium can be punctured or destroyed much more easily than true adamantium, but still requires a massive amount of force to be damaged.

THE THANOS EFFECT

DURABILITY
Very few things have proven stronger than this miracle metal. The alloy can withstand significant force, and even survive a direct hit from a nuclear weapon. In fact, the only compound known to pierce this metal is a rare substance called Antarctic vibranium. However, adamantium has proved susceptible to magic and other mystical forces. During the struggle for the Infinity Gauntlet, the mad Titan Thanos turned Logan's adamantium-laced bones to spongy rubber.

Adamantium is Wolverine's secret weapon, his ace in the hole. It's the literal backbone of his every action.

Anatomy of a Hero

Wolverine's claws are made of bone, so the adamantium bonded to them as well as to his skeleton.

The adamantium bonding process left every bone in Wolverine's body coated in the near-indestructible alloy.

One of the few individuals capable of surviving the adamantium bonding process, Wolverine has since learned to embrace the metal, relying on it to increase the impact of his own attacks, as well as lessen the effects of attacks on his person.

CLAW DETAIL
Bone claws (later coated with adamantium) can slice through most materials.

Claws break skin every time they are popped.

Could it be older than first thought?

APOCALYPSE LINK? During an escapade referred to as the Jungle Adventure, Wolverine defeated one of Apocalypse's android doppelgangers. While exploring the mutant overlord's ancient base, Logan discovered a mysterious and still unexplained adamantium skull.

Does anyone else have it?

Though a truly rare alloy, adamantium plays many roles in the Marvel Universe. For a time, even Wolverine's hated enemy Sabretooth had the metal bonded to his own skeleton.

* Agent Zero's combat knife
* The outer skin of some of Alkhema's robotic bodies
* Battlestar's shield
* Bullseye's spinal column and some strips coating several of his bones
* Constrictor's original, wrist-mounted, prehensile metal coils
* Cyber's claws and armor
* A unique set of Doctor Octopus's arms
* Hammerhead's skull plate
* The outer layer of Citizen V's rapier
* Lady Deathstrike's skeleton and talons
* One of Mister Fantastic's labs for extremely dangerous experiments
* Moon Knight's crescent blades
* A unique suit of armor once used by the villain Stilt-Man
* The outer skin of TESS-One
* The outer skin of some of Ultron's robotic bodies
* X-23's claws
* One of several layers of containment at the superhuman incarceration facility known as the Vault
* An outer coating on the Swordsman's blades
* A special brand of bullet in the Iron Man suit's ballistic weapons

RUNNING WILD

Logan had always been a hunter, but the Weapon X project had made him into a true predator.

He had survived the adamantium bonding process. He had survived the memory implants and the constant poking and prodding. With the help of his healing factor, Logan could survive most anything. The problem was, he hadn't survived as a man. The artificial metal skeleton that now made up his frame had poisoned his mind and reduced him to his most feral state, forcing him to roam the Canadian wild as the animal he had become.

THE HUNTER IN DARKNESS

There were other predators lurking in the woods. The Hunter in Darkness had long been a popular piece of Canadian folklore. A giant, wolf-like beast that stood on two legs, the Hunter made his home in the wilds of Wood Buffalo National Park in Northern Alberta, not far from where Logan had been born. So it was almost inevitable that the two would cross paths when Logan, in his feral state, instinctively retreated to his old stomping grounds. Finding the creature caught in a bear trap, Logan's compassionate human side showed through his primitive state, and he set the injured beast free, earning himself a future ally when, as Wolverine, Logan would encounter the Hunter later in his troubled life.

RETURN OF THE Native

She was a face from Wolverine's past that he couldn't recall. But he knew her scent well, and her touch even better.

She had been his chosen mate years ago. The wild woman known only as the Native had survived the Experiment X program with Logan, and reunited with her fellow test subject sometime after his escape in a small cabin in the Pacific Northwest. The two had lived modestly and happily, not unlike Logan's years with Silver Fox. Of course the difference was, he couldn't remember any of it.

And he wouldn't for years. Long after his time in the wild, long after he had joined up with his fellow mutants the X-Men, Logan and his former lover rekindled their romance. And, ironically, Sabretooth was responsible. When Sabretooth was hired by a corrupt company to track down and capture the Native, he realized he couldn't do the job alone. So he revealed her existence to Wolverine, knowing his pint-sized nemesis couldn't resist the chance to find out more about his own past (**1**). A much better tracker than his foe, Logan quickly located the Native (**2**), but ended up fighting with the feral creature when she remembered his fierce behavior during the Experiment X procedure (**3**). As their violence led to animal lust, the two mutants found familiar comfort in each other's arms (**4**), before the Native took Logan back to the cabin that they had once shared many years ago.

However their reunion would be short-lived. Leading his employer's operatives to Logan's door (**5**), Sabretooth and his associates attacked the couple, briefly imprisoning the Native (**6**) until Wolverine helped her escape back into the wild (**7**), (**8**). Angered by Logan's interference, Sabretooth then hunted and murdered the Native, ending yet another of Wolverine's romances in cold blood.

"YEAH, YOU KEEP RUNNING RUNT. YOU AND YOUR LITTLE PUPPY GIRL..."

SABRETOOTH

DEPARTMENT H

The brainchild of Canadian government agent and former petrochemical engineer James Hudson, Department H was a top-secret research and development agency established by Canada's Ministry of Defense. Department H consisted of Hudson, his wife Heather, and Wolverine, whom the couple had discovered roaming the wilds of Wood Buffalo National Park. Department H broadened its horizons after Hudson was impressed by the American Super Hero team the Fantastic Four. Hudson created a group called Alpha Flight, making Wolverine team leader after he showed his capabilities during a battle with the villain Egghead. However, Logan hated working for the government and joined Professor X's X-Men instead.

CANADA'S FIRST LINE OF DEFENSE, ALPHA FLIGHT, STANDS AS THE COUNTRY'S PREMIER SUPER HERO TEAM—ONE THAT HAS LASTED THROUGH MANY INCARNATIONS.

BETA & GAMMA

In an attempt to make Alpha Flight a fluid organism—ever growing, expanding, and evolving—Department H also developed other divisions of their Flight program. These smaller factions were meant as testing grounds for heroes, and the program evolved into a three-tier system. The lowest rung, Gamma Flight, consisted of untrained heroes, including the likes of future Wolverine enemy Wild Child. Beta Flight were their upperclassmen, the players nearly ready for prime time. And, of course, at the top of the hierarchy sat Alpha Flight—the ultimate goal of every hero enrolled in Department H.

WENDIGO

During one of Wolverine's first missions with Department H, he was instructed to bring down the rampaging brute known as the Hulk. But the battle also led him into conflict with the Wendigo, a cannibalistic creature haunting the Canadian wilderness. Later, Logan would get another crack at the wild albino beast when venturing back to Canada in order to clear his name with Alpha Flight. His former team was still angry with him for abandoning his post and Logan wanted to make peace with his old friends. During his trip, Wolverine helped Alpha Frlight to locate a missing boy. And in doing so, he ran smack into the Wendigo.

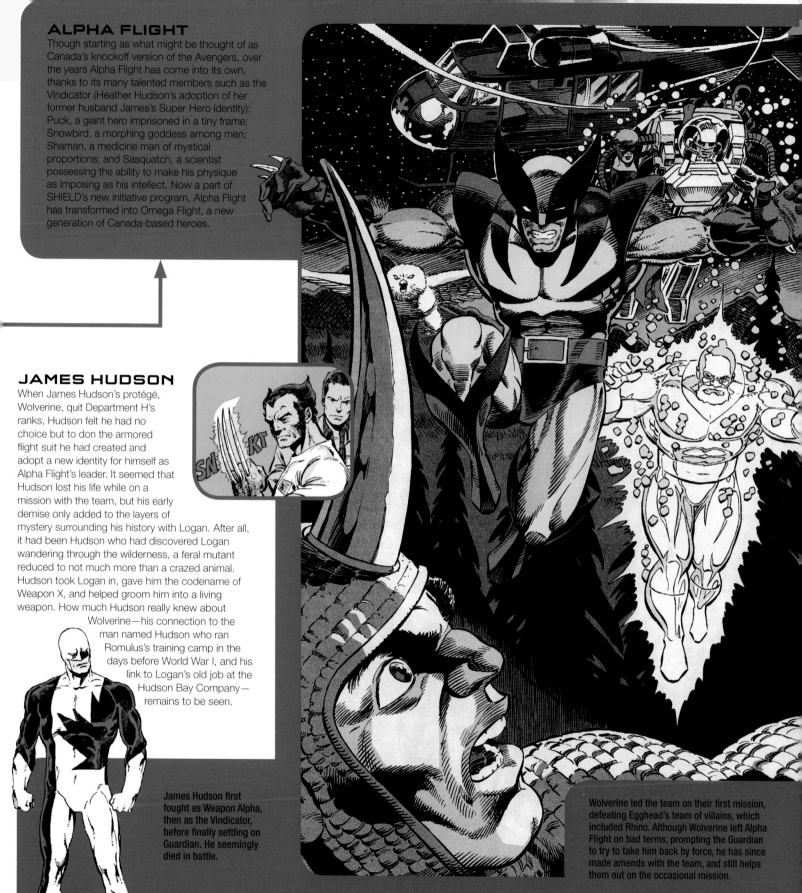

ALPHA FLIGHT

Though starting as what might be thought of as Canada's knockoff version of the Avengers, over the years Alpha Flight has come into its own, thanks to its many talented members such as the Vindicator (Heather Hudson's adoption of her former husband James's Super Hero identity); Puck, a giant hero imprisoned in a tiny frame; Snowbird, a morphing goddess among men; Shaman, a medicine man of mystical proportions; and Sasquatch, a scientist possessing the ability to make his physique as imposing as his intellect. Now a part of SHIELD's new initiative program, Alpha Flight has transformed into Omega Flight, a new generation of Canada-based heroes.

JAMES HUDSON

When James Hudson's protégé, Wolverine, quit Department H's ranks, Hudson felt he had no choice but to don the armored flight suit he had created and adopt a new identity for himself as Alpha Flight's leader. It seemed that Hudson lost his life while on a mission with the team, but his early demise only added to the layers of mystery surrounding his history with Logan. After all, it had been Hudson who had discovered Logan wandering through the wilderness, a feral mutant reduced to not much more than a crazed animal. Hudson took Logan in, gave him the codename of Weapon X, and helped groom him into a living weapon. How much Hudson really knew about Wolverine—his connection to the man named Hudson who ran Romulus's training camp in the days before World War I, and his link to Logan's old job at the Hudson Bay Company— remains to be seen.

James Hudson first fought as Weapon Alpha, then as the Vindicator, before finally settling on Guardian. He seemingly died in battle.

Wolverine led the team on their first mission, defeating Egghead's team of villains, which included Rhino. Although Wolverine left Alpha Flight on bad terms, prompting the Guardian to try to take him back by force, he has since made amends with the team, and still helps them out on the occasional mission.

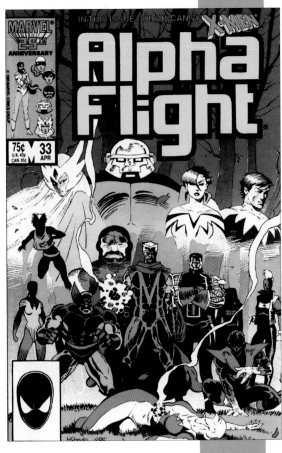

Publication date
April 1986

Editor-in-chief
Jim Shooter

Cover artist
Mike Mignola

Writer
Bill Mantlo

Penciller
Sal Buscema

Inker
Gerry Talaoc

Colorist
Bob Sharen

Letterer
Jim Novak

ALPHA FLIGHT #33

"That 'thing' is some kind of man, Heather!"

James Hudson, a.k.a. Guardian

MAIN CHARACTERS: Guardian (Heather Hudson), Marrina, Snowbird, Aurora, Northstar, Puck, Box, Madison Jeffries, Wolverine, James Hudson, Lady Deathstrike
SUPPORTING CHARACTERS: Namor, Attuma, Corporal Thomson, Storm, Colossus, Rachel Summers, Kitty Pryde, Rogue, Nightcrawler, Magneto
LOCATIONS: Quebec, Canada; Westchester, New York; McKenzie District, Northwest Territory, Canada; San Juan De Fuca, British Columbia, Canada; Wood Buffalo National Park, Canada

Background

Wolverine's past was still pretty much a mystery, and his fans were chomping at the bit. In 1986, as the comics industry began to discover a sizeable market for mature storytelling, Wolverine was rising to the top of the Marvel pantheon. The hidden depths of his character attracted more and more top talent. Wolverine began to star in guest appearances across Marvel's line, giving writer Bill Mantlo a chance to play with the character once more when he popped up in a two-part story starting in *Alpha Flight #33*. Mantlo had established his name with Marvel's *Micronauts* series, a licensed property that gave him freedom to indulge his imagination, creating worlds on top of worlds. Mantlo had even teamed the X-Men with the Micronauts in a four-issue 1984 miniseries, spotlighting two of Marvel's most popular teams.

When working on this milestone issue of *Alpha Flight*, Mantlo was accompanied by rising star Mike Mignola, previously of the book's interior pages, who decorated the cover of each issue in his trademark style. Mignola would go on to superstardom after creating the character Hellboy for Dark Horse Comics, his innovative, impressionist style influencing generations of comic-book artists to come.

The Story

Wolverine is paid a visit by the Guardian, Heather Hudson, who reveals how Logan came to join Alpha Flight in his years before the X-Men...

1

2

"I never said I wouldn't help you, beautiful! I just said you were nuts!"

3

4

Heather Hudson longed to make a name for herself. One of the founding members of the Canadian Super Hero team Alpha Flight, Heather felt she was merely a support for her husband James MacDonald Hudson who, when wearing an enhanced battlesuit, was the Flight's team leader, the Guardian. When her husband died in combat, Heather decided to adopt a version of the costume for herself and serve her nation just as her husband had before her **(1)**. There was just one problem: she lacked the fighting skills for her desired profession.

That's where Wolverine came in. Knowing Logan from his past with Alpha Flight, Heather decided to fly to Westchester, New York, to request training from her old friend. However, as she approached the X-Men's secret home at the Xavier School For Gifted Youngsters, she did not think to announce her arrival before rocketing herself onto the school's grounds. Thinking they were under attack, the X-Men knocked the fledgling hero out of the sky **(2)**. After Wolverine realized the group's error, he convinced his teammates to leave his unconscious friend in his care. The team agreed, after recognizing the identity of their supposed attacker.

Meanwhile, across the Hudson River, an ominous-looking woman was approaching, tracking the adamantium in Wolverine's bones. Her name was Lady Deathstrike, a figure from the hero Daredevil's past. Deathstrike had murdered her father, Lord Dark Wind, in a matter of honor, and she was seeking out the recipients of the adamantium-bonding process her father had perfected. The formula for this had been stolen from him by an unknown party years before. Deathstrike had locked on to Wolverine's signal, and she had hired a small army of samurai to take back what she believed to be rightfully hers.

Having agreed to help train Heather Hudson **(3)**, Wolverine began to reminisce about the time he first met the young heroine. Years earlier, after fleeing the corrupt Weapon X Program, Wolverine attacked a young couple named James and Heather Hudson who were honeymooning in a cabin in Canada's Wood Buffalo National Park. Not much more than a feral wild animal, Wolverine pounced on the couple, despite receiving a shotgun blast from James. Heather finally put Wolverine out of commission with another shotgun shell **(4)**. She and James then took him back to their cabin. James was fascinated by the mutant, realizing that he could be of value to his employers Department H, a branch of the Canadian secret service. James hiked back down the mountain to find help for Wolverine's wounds, leaving Heather alone with Wolverine. As a blizzard raged, delaying James, Wolverine's mutant healing factor began to work. In a moment of fevered frenzy, Wolverine popped his adamantium claws. Instead of fleeing, Heather took pity on Logan, realizing that he must have been the victim of some twisted lab experiment **(5)**, and held him in her arms until James returned. In a debt of gratitude, Wolverine subsequently went to work for James in the Canadian government's Department H program, a job that Logan only quit after he began to develop feelings for Heather deeper than friendship.

Back in the present, Wolverine and Heather's reunion was cut short when they found themselves surrounded by Lady Deathstrike and her men **(6)**. In a battle spilling into the pages of *Alpha Flight #34*, Wolverine and Heather bested the samurai, Heather adopting the new Super Hero codename of Vindicator in the process. Realizing she was much more prepared for her life as a hero than she had thought, Heather left Westchester and returned to Canada, leaving behind Wolverine and his unresolved feelings for her.

5

"Those claws aren't you, are they? Somebody did that to you!"

6

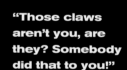

WOLVERINE VS. THE HULK

ONE IS THE BEST THERE IS AT WHAT HE DOES; THE OTHER IS THE STRONGEST ONE THERE IS. DESPITE THEIR CLAIMS, WOLVERINE AND THE HULK HAVE BEEN FIGHTING A STALEMATE FOR YEARS.

On one of his first missions for the Canadian government's Department H, Wolverine was assigned to take down the Hulk. Since that day, the two have rarely passed up an opportunity to resume their battle for supremacy. With the Hulk's volatile temper and Wolverine's need to see a job through to the end, their rivalry seems permanent, with no clear-cut victor.

Wolverine and the Hulk have clashed everywhere from the heartland of America's wildernesses to the villain Nightmare's dream-like private island. And time and time again, the Hulk has shown an innate ability to provoke Wolverine into a berserker frenzy, a side of his personality that Wolverine would rather not reveal, given the choice.

UNEASY ALLIES

Sparring partners frequently develop a grudging camaraderie, and Wolverine and the Hulk are no exceptions. Despite their many clashes, the two heroes have reluctantly joined forces several times.

When the Hulk visited Madripoor years ago, he teamed up with Logan's alter ego Patch. The Hulk never realized that his old rival was helping him take down a parasitic drug dealer.

On another occasion, the two teamed up to help bring the former X-Man and shape-shifter Mimic to justice, after an unhinged Mimic had taken Logan's form and embarked on a crime spree.

Over the years, Wolverine and the Hulk have grown to have mutual respect for one another, so much so that during the cosmic events revolving around the creation of the mystical Infinity Gauntlet, the Hulk and Wolverine shared a few quiet moments of reflection. Meanwhile, the world around them was thrown into chaos, creating a rare situation in which these two mighty heroes suddenly felt completely powerless.

"IN OUR OWN WAYS, WE'RE BOTH MONSTERS."

WORLD WAR HULK

The Hulk is literally fueled by anger. The madder he gets, the stronger he becomes. When he was exiled to another planet by Earth's heroes, he got more than a little perturbed. Nevertheless, he managed to make the best of it, conquering the world in his name and even falling in love and taking a bride. But when his adopted planet was all but blown to pieces by a bomb that the Hulk mistakenly assumed had been set by those same heroes, he returned to Earth madder than he had ever been. Easily overpowering nearly all of his Super Hero contemporaries, the Hulk stormed Xavier's school in Westchester, thinking Professor X might have been partially to blame for the destruction of his newly adopted world. Despite Xavier having had nothing to do with the tragedy, the enraged Hulk became involved in a bruising battle with the X-Men, with Wolverine fearlessly charging into the fray. This time, the Hulk was so angry, the battle was no contest. He swatted Wolverine away as if he were an annoying bug.

GRAY AREA

Like Wolverine, the Hulk has undergone many transformations over the years. When Dr. Bruce Banner was first hit with the gamma explosion that changed him into the Hulk, he originally appeared as a shade of gray. As different multiple personalities inside Banner's mind began to take turns piloting the Hulk, his outside hue changed. The Hulk shifted from gray to green and back again, as the monster changed from mean-spirited creature, to mindless beast, to scheming brute. The one thing the Hulk's different personalities have in common is that they've all battled Wolverine.

CHAPTER **THREE**

Wolverine and the X-Men

X-MEN MEMBERS

PROFESSOR X

Charles Xavier, also known as Professor X, is the founder and guiding voice behind the X-Men Super Hero team. A mutant himself, he initially used his School for Gifted Youngsters in Westchester, New York as a cover for secretly training young mutants. Xavier later went public, revealing to the world his vast psychic abilities and quickly becoming a respected authority on mutants.

SHADOWCAT

Katherine "Kitty" Pryde has been known by many names over the years—Ariel, Sprite, Shadowcat, and Kitten, to name a few. Just like her name, Kitty's personality has changed too. Once a wide-eyed pupil at Professor X's School for Gifted Youngsters, she is now an invaluable team player and dedicated teacher. Thanks to her mutant abilities she is able to shift through solid matter.

NIGHTCRAWLER

Although his close friend Wolverine often refers to him affectionately as "Elf," Kurt Wagner is more than capable of holding his own in any X-Men fight. Able to teleport himself, or even a few others from one location to the next with merely a thought, Nightcrawler is as evasive as he is surprising in the field of battle.

COLOSSUS

Already quite imposing at a hulking 6ft 6in, Piotr Rasputin becomes downright intimidating when he uses his mutant abilities to increase his size and mass. He is able to transform his body tissue into a nearly unbreakable steel-like organic material, and gains super-strength as a result of this metamorphosis.

WOLVERINE

Joining the X-Men during their crucial mission to the mutant island Krakoa, Wolverine found a family as well as a team while fighting beside his fellow mutants. Although he will always find the need to indulge in a solo mission now and again, Logan has long ago acknowledged that he will keep returning to the X-Men for the rest of his life.

JUBILEE

Serving as Logan's surrogate daughter and sidekick for a time, Jubilation Lee used her firework-like mutant pyrotechnics, her street smarts, and her upbeat attitude to fight alongside the X-Men as well as Generation X. She eventually lost her mutant abilities during the House of M event, and joined up with the underground hero team the New Warriors, using advanced technology to become the hero known as Wondra.

ARCHANGEL

Warren Worthington III, another of the X-Men's founding members, changed from a rich teen heartthrob into the hated and feared high-flying mutant Angel. After undergoing a transformation by the evil mutant overlord Apocalypse, Warren adopted the identity of Archangel, the moniker somehow seeming a better fit for his now harder image.

CYCLOPS

He was the X-Men's first leader, and he has rarely relinquished that title since. Having recently accepted even more responsibility after taking over Professor X's position, Scott Summers continues to use his shrewd mind and concussive eye blasts to guide the X-Men's future.

Although he usually prefers to work alone, Wolverine has come to realize that sometimes teamwork is the only option. When six claws and a bad attitude just aren't enough, Logan partners with his fellow mutants of the amazing X-Men.

ROGUE

Although her past is largely a mystery, it is known that Anna Marie was raised by the mutants Mystique and Destiny, and that she embarked on a criminal life before changing sides and joining the X-Men. Possessing super-strength as well as the ability to absorb the powers and energy of others, Rogue has more than made up for her past sins during her time with the X-Men.

ICEMAN

Robert "Bobby" Drake was one of the original X-Men, but often felt out of place because he was the team's youngest member. Today, Bobby displays expert control over his mutant ice projecting powers, and serves as an inspiration to the young mutants of the Xavier Institute for Higher Learning (as the School for Gifted Youngsters is now known.)

STORM

Although she is the new bride of the hero known as the Black Panther, and therefore the queen of the African nation of Wakanda, Ororo Iquadi T'Challa (née Munroe) is an old hand to the ranks of the X-Men. She has lent her mutant weather-manipulation abilities in many a battle.

BEAST

Henry "Hank" McCoy has been evolving his whole life. A former child prodigy and a scientist by inclination, as the X-Men's Beast, Hank has changed from being an agile man with large feet, to a furry humanoid blue creature, to his current secondary mutation as a lion-like renaissance man.

PHOENIX

The heart and soul of the X-Men from the very beginning, Jean Grey took a piece of every one of her teammates with her when she died. A formidable telepath with telekinetic skills as well, Jean always struggled to contain the cosmic power of the Phoenix force, a battle she endured until the day she died.

HAVOK

Always feeling second best to his brother Cyclops, Alex Summers nonetheless became an important part of the X-Men, even leading the team on occasion. Possessing the ability to fire concussive blasts of plasma out of his hands, Havok continues his on-again/off-again relationship with both the mutant team and his girlfriend Polaris.

GAMBIT

Born in the bayou of Louisiana, Remy LeBeau possesses a unique outlook on life—one that has gotten him into quite a lot of trouble with the law as well as with women. Despite his lapses, Remy normally uses his energy-charging abilities for the greater good.

WHITE QUEEN

Formerly the headmistress of the Massachusetts Academy and Professor X's chief rival in recruiting new mutant finds, Emma Frost has since reformed her ways, and lends her impressive telepathic abilities to the X-Men, as well as to her lover, Scott Summers.

OLVERINE'S X-MEN FOE

MAGNETO

Eric Magnus Lehnsherr grew up in a Nazi death camp. He survived the ordeal and was left with a lifelong appreciation for his fellow mutants. His violent campaign to see mutants freed from human oppression has brought him into conflict with the X-Men many times, but his mastery of magnetism has always kept them at bay.

MR. SINISTER

Nathaniel Essex was given the name Sinister by the mutant overlord Apocalypse when the two crossed paths in the 19th century. A brilliant geneticist and strategist, Mr. Sinister was a thorn in the X-Men's side until his murder at the hands of the shape-shifting Mystique.

SEBASTIAN SHAW

The Black King of Manhattan's clandestine Hellfire Club, Sebastian Shaw led a campaign against the X-Men, kidnapping Jean Grey in the process. Although he has been defeated time and again by the heroes, Shaw nevertheless continues to utilize his kinetic energy redirection powers to challenge his foes.

JUGGERNAUT

Cain Marko thought that when he was originally granted super-strength and invulnerability by the mystical Crimson Gem of the Cyttorak, that he could finally end his rivalry with his stepbrother Charles Xavier. Yet somehow, all the behemoth managed to achieve was defeat at the hands of the X-Men.

CASSANDRA NOVA

One of the bodiless parasites known as Mummudrai, Cassandra Nova copied Charles Xavier's DNA while he was in the womb, bringing herself into the physical world as his twin sister. As an adult, she set out to destroy all mutants, and even caused the destruction of the nation of Genosha.

MASTERMIND

Although now deceased, Jason Wyngarde was a formidable mutant in his time, using his abilities to manipulate others to see and hear what he wished them to. At his prime, he even influenced Jean Grey into joining the corrupt Hellfire Club as his lover.

STRYFE

The clone of the mutant Cable, Stryfe embarked on a mission to destroy his would-be family, consisting of Cable's father, Cyclops, and his X-Men teammates. A powerful telekinetic mutant, Stryfe was rewarded for his cruel ways with an untimely death.

THE SENTINELS

The brainchildren of mechanical genius Bolivar Trask, the giant robots called the Sentinels were originally created to put an end to mutant life everywhere. Having gone through several upgrades over the years, ironically now a handful of Sentinels are used by the government to protect mutant life.

While Wolverine has amassed an impressive rogues' gallery in his personal life, most villains can't hold a candle to the dire universal threats he's faced during his time with the X-Men.

DARK PHOENIX

A duplicate of Jean Grey's body, and possessing a shred of the female mutant's conscience, the Dark Phoenix was a force of nature, destroying an entire solar system before it committed suicide after convincing itself and the X-Men that it was truly the heroine Jean Grey.

BLACK TOM CASSIDY

The brother of former X-Man Banshee, Black Tom Cassidy was the black sheep of the family. Having transformed from a mutant able to generate concussive blasts into a plant-manipulating master and back again, Black Tom still continues his vendetta with the X-Men despite his brother's death.

THE BLOB

Although he lost his powers on M-Day in the wake of the House of M event, Fred J. Dukes had been a longtime member of the Brotherhood of Evil Mutants, utilizing his enormous girth and immovable weight to constantly stand in the X-Men's way.

ARCADE

Obsessed with video games of all varieties, paid assassin Arcade has used his genius level intellect and his penchant for technology and design to run the X-Men through his various gauntlets in his Murderworlds, deadly theme parks that seemingly bring video games to life.

BASTION

The combination of the artificial intelligence of the future Sentinel Nimrod and the Sentinel Master Mold, Bastion took on a human form, and began to follow his original programming in a campaign against all mutants, even manipulating a faction of the US government to help him in his cause.

MOJO

The undisputed ruler of Mojoworld, Mojo runs his media-obsessed dimension with a remote of iron, constantly using the X-Men and other earthlings as pawns in his demented movie productions and reality TV experiments, not caring if his "actors" live to see the season finale.

GOBLYN QUEEN

An identical clone of Jean Grey, Madelyne Pryor was birthed in Mr. Sinister's labs, and was quickly accepted by a heartbroken Cyclops as a replacement for his seemingly dead lover, Jean. After giving birth to Cyclops's son Cable, Madelyne soon revealed her truly demented colors when Jean Grey resurfaced.

DANGER

When the X-Men's complex training facility known as the Danger Room slowly gained a mind of her own, Danger was born, a cybernetic life form able to exploit the limitations and fighting nuances of the entire X-Men team she knows so well.

WOLVERINE AND JEAN GREY

He was attracted to her right away. Possessing a kind soul and a resemblance to Logan's first love, Rose, Jean Grey quickly became the object of his unrequited affection.

When first they met, Jean didn't much care for Logan's attitude or for the nickname of "Jeannie" that he gave her, but she slowly warmed to him.

Early years

From the beginning, she was somebody else's girl. By the time Wolverine joined the X-Men, the telepathic Jean Grey and Scott Summers, aka Cyclops, had been in a relationship for years. So when Logan developed a crush on the young woman who called herself Marvel Girl, he didn't stand much chance of winning her heart.

But when Jean seemingly died on a mission to space only to be reborn as the powerful Phoenix, Logan decided to make his affections known. However, he thought better of it when he realized how many other people cared for the young woman and instead decided to bury his feelings deep inside himself. But things weren't as they seemed. Jean grew more and more powerful until she almost appeared to be a different entity entirely.

The insidious Hellfire Club kidnapped Jean, subjecting her to mind control, and the Jean Grey the X-Men knew and loved was no more.

"HEAR ME, X-MEN!
NO LONGER AM I THE WOMAN YOU KNEW!
I AM FIRE! AND LIFE INCARNATE! NOW AND FOREVER"

--I AM PHOENIX!

BOOM!

The Birth of Phoenix

It turned out that a cosmic entity had merged with Jean Grey. With her all-too human emotions corrupting the Phoenix Force within her, Jean Grey became the Dark Phoenix, and carved a path of destruction throughout the cosmos, even obliterating an entire solar system. With the help of the alien Shi'ar race, the X-Men fought the Phoenix for a time, allowing Jean Grey's tortured personality to emerge if only for a moment. Realizing the scope of what she had done, Jean took her own life, and thus saved the entire universe.

However, as the X-Men would come to learn, the Phoenix that had died that day was not Jean Grey. In fact, the real Jean had been in a cocoon of sorts at the bottom of Jamaica Bay—the place she had apparently been reborn as the Phoenix all those months ago. At that time, the cosmic entity of the Phoenix Force had tapped into her potential power, and made itself into her doppelganger, its performance so perfect, even the Force believed itself to be the real deal.

Fooled by the Phoenix Force's duplicate into thinking she was their friend Jean Grey, the X-Men were truly devastated by Jean's apparent betrayal and then her death.

"D-DO IT, WOLVERINE!"

Love and Marriage

Resurrected and returned to her place beside the founding X-Men in the newly formed team X-Factor, Jean Grey's return shocked her longtime friends. As X-Factor soon rejoined with their fellow mutants of the X-Men, Jean resumed her relationship with Cyclops, although she could not deny her attraction to the feral Logan. The two even shared a few fleeting moments of passion during the life-threatening situation known as the Inferno event, where Manhattan became a literal hell on Earth, as well as during the X-Tinction Agenda, when Jean believed Logan to be dying while locked in a prison. But in the end, Jean always chose Cyclops, and finally, the two were married. Although he could not bring himself to attend the ceremony, Wolverine nevertheless watched the proceedings from afar, with a small part of himself even happy for his two old friends.

The Death of Jean Grey

Lured by the demented mutant Xorn onto an Asteroid satellite that was then hurled towards the sun, Wolverine and Jean Grey realized they had no chance of escape. As their quarters began to slowly get hotter and hotter, Jean could no longer stand the pain, and asked for Logan to end her life with his claws. Obliging his love her last wish, Jean's death unlocked the power of the Phoenix once more. Thus empowered, Jean returned Logan and herself to Earth, as Logan slowly healed from being burned alive.

However, as the duo confronted Xorn alongside their fellow X-Men, Xorn injected Jean with a lethal electromagnetic pulse and she died in her husband's arms.

WOLVERINE
AND THE X-MEN

With only one solo adventure to his credit, Wolverine didn't find his true home until he was enlisted by Professor X into the elaborate world of the X-Men.

A handshake sealed the deal. Recruited by the X-Men's founder Professor Charles Xavier on a mission to rescue the original X-Men members, Wolverine became an integral part of the mutant team's second generation. As members of the old guard moved on to new adventures, leaving only Cyclops and Marvel Girl behind to train the band of newcomers, Wolverine found himself part of something much larger than he originally anticipated. At first, Wolverine masked his true emotions beneath his trademark cowboy hat, opting to play the role of the runt with a chip on his shoulder and something to prove. He slowly developed into a proud team player, even orchestrating coordinated attacks with his other teammates, like his famous "fastball special," where Colossus would pick him up and literally pitch him at their intended target. Little by little, Logan began to reveal more and more of his true personality to the X-Men, even as he started to fall in love with Cyclops's girlfriend, his teammate Jean Grey. Wolverine's feelings towards the mutant telepath also known as Marvel Girl only helped to strengthen the animosity Wolverine and Cyclops had felt since their first meeting. Indeed while Wolverine was quickly becoming a close friend of Nightcrawler and Colossus, he and Cyclops would never see eye to eye.

"I've just about had it with your 'MAD KILLER' act, pal."

Logan always struggled to keep his bestial side in check, but sometimes it resurfaced and caused trouble between himself and his teammates.

Wolverine's feelings for Jean Grey blossomed when she supposedly died and was reborn as the Phoenix. However, he pushed his feelings to the back of his mind, the activities of numerous Super Villains keeping him occupied. During this era, Wolverine and the X-Men tangled with Professor X's hulking stepbrother Juggernaut, teammate Banshee's scheming brother Black Tom Cassidy, and of course, the master of magnetism, Magneto. The team also faced robotic duplicates of the original X-Men and the cosmic power of Firelord, and journeyed into space to meet the alien race known as the Shi'ar. The X-Men proved their loyalty to Wolverine when they chose to stick by his side even after Guardian, calling himself Weapon Alpha, of Canada's Department H, attempted to drag Wolverine back to his native country.

"It's NO ACT, leader-man."

X-Men #106 (Aug. 1977)
After their teammate Thunderbird's death, Cyclops began to drive the team harder than usual, an action Wolverine refused to tolerate.

X-Men #107 (Oct. 1977)
Traveling into space to battle the Shi'ar aliens, Wolverine was forced to don a brown and tan costume belonging to savage alien Fang when his own uniform was shredded.

X-Men #109 (Feb. 1978)
Wolverine battled James Hudson with the help of the X-Men, when his old friend tried to force him to return to Canada's Department H program.

GIANT-SIZE X-MEN

MARVEL COMICS GROUP.

1 1975 02940

50¢

68 BIG PAGES

GIANT-SIZE X-MEN

SENSES SHATTERING 1st ISSUE!

NEW! DEADLY GENESIS!

Publication date
May 1975

Editor-in-chief
Len Wein

Cover artist
Gil Kane

Writer
Len Wein

Penciller
Dave Cockrum

Inker
Gil Kane

Colorist
Glyn Johns

Letterer
John Costanza

Giant-Size X-Men #1

"From the ashes of the past there grow the fires of the future!"

MAIN CHARACTERS: Professor X, Cyclops, Wolverine, Nightcrawler, Banshee, Storm, Sunfire, Colossus, Thunderbird, Krakoa
SUPPORTING CHARACTERS: Marvel Girl, Iceman, Angel, Havok, Polaris, Illyana Rasputin, Alexandra Rasputin, Nikolai Rasputin, Beast (cover only)
LOCATIONS: Winzeldorf, Germany; Quebec, Canada; Nashville, Tennessee; Kenya, East Africa; Osaka, Japan; Lake Baikal, Siberia; Camp Verde, Arizona; Westchester, New York; Krakoa, South Pacific

Background

Wolverine was getting a makeover whether he needed one or not. With only three comic appearances under his belt (*The Incredible Hulk #180-182*), Wolverine had barely gone public, and hardly deserved a revamp. However, when legendary artist Gil Kane pencilled the cover to the special *Giant-Size X-Men #1*, he incorrectly rendered Wolverine's costume, omitting the whiskers from Logan's introductory appearance, and adding longer, pointed "ears" on his headpiece. The book's interior artist, Dave Cockrum, loved the changes, thinking they gave the character an edgier look similar to DC Comics' Batman, and the altered uniform became canon, Wolverine wearing it as late as the 2000s.

But Logan's appearance was only a fraction of the excitement created by this landmark special issue. With the X-Men title in reprint limbo for the previous few years, *Giant-Size X-Men* marked the rebirth of the team, and the beginning of an era still remembered today as the X-Men's heyday.

When the X-Men are taken captive on a mission, their founder, Professor Charles Xavier, is forced to mount a rescue attempt by forming a new incarnation of the heroic team...

Life had never been easy for mutants. It was a fact that Kurt Wagner, the blue-hued teleporter called Nightcrawler, was quickly discovering as he fled an angry horde of his fellow German villagers. Overcome by the bloodthirsty angry mob, Kurt was shocked to find his attackers suddenly frozen in a trance-like state, courtesy of Professor Charles Xavier (**1**). Also known as telepathic Professor X, Xavier had sought out Nightcrawler, wishing the young mutant's aid on a mysterious mission.

After signing Kurt up for his cause, Xavier's next stop was Quebec, Canada, where he successfully recruited Wolverine, a top secret agent who saw the X-Men as his chance to operate without the constraints of a domineering military institution (**2**). Afterwards, Professor X continued his recruitment drive by heading to Tennessee to speak with the sonic-screaming Banshee; Africa, to have an audience with the weather-controlling Storm; and Japan, to meet with the solar-powered Sunfire. And after also enrolling the metal-plated Colossus and the super-strong Native American Thunderbird, Professor X assembled his new team of X-Men at his mansion in Westchester, New York, in order to brief them on a danger so dire, it would require all of their various combined talents to combat it.

With his audience growing restless, Professor X gave the floor to Cyclops, the field leader of his original X-Men team (**3**). And that's when Cyclops dropped the bombshell. He'd led a team consisting of the telepathic Marvel Girl, his brother the plasma-firing Havok, the magnetic manipulator Polaris, the winged aviator Angel, and the aptly named Iceman to a mysterious island in the South Pacific called Krakoa. The island had registered an off-the-charts power reading on Professor X's mutant locating Cerebro device, so the team had rocketed off to Krakoa to meet this impressive new member of their *homo superior* race. Once they had landed, the group was hit by a tremendous force (**4**), and Cyclops found himself alone on the jet, heading back to New York against his will. The new X-Men that the Professor had recruited would become his new strike force, members of a rescue operation whose only goal was to locate Cyclops's missing team.

With his new X-Men in tow, Cyclops jetted back to Krakoa, immediately facing a myriad of threats, including attacking vines, rockslides, and giant sea creatures. The team discovered an ancient temple and, to their horror, found their missing allies hooked to a web of tubes that were draining the mutants' life forces. Cyclops and his team freed the X-men prisoners, only to have Angel inform him that that was what their unseen enemy wanted. Their enemy had supped on the X-Men and now desired a second serving; Cyclops had unwittingly delivered that very thing. At that moment, the X-Men's enemy revealed himself. He wasn't a powerful being living on the island of Krakoa at all. The island *itself* was the mutant (**5**).

With the X-Men past and present united against their common foe (**6**), Professor X used his telepathic powers to inform the team of a weak point he'd deduced in Krakoa's makeup. At Cyclops's command, Storm channeled lightning from the heavens into the body of Polaris, who used her energies to sever Krakoa from the Earth, propelling the island mutant into outer space (**7**). The team managed to escape the resulting whirlpool unharmed, wondering what the future held for their newly formed band of mutants.

2

3

4

"I'm ashamed to say I never even saw what hit us!"

5

6

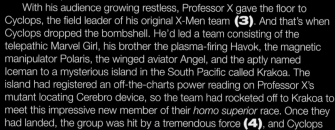

7

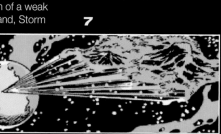

WOLVERINE
AND THE X-MEN

Wolverine was growing up. Comics were becoming more sophisticated, and Logan was following suit, his character gaining a whole new level of depth.

As the decade began, Logan slowly began to grab more moments in the spotlight. His past a well-guarded secret, he nevertheless grew closer to his teammates. His unrequited love for Jean Grey resurfaced, and he watched the object of his affection undergo brainwashing by the notorious Mastermind of the evil elite Hellfire Club. This deviant programming corrupted Jean's already fragile mind and the former heroine transformed into the evil entity known as Dark Phoenix. Wolverine was forced to help the X-Men battle her, as she had grown so powerful that her mere existence threatened the entire universe. But in a brief moment of clarity, Jean realized the errors of her ways and killed herself, forcing Logan to watch his love die yet again. As the years continued, Wolverine faced the demons of his past while clearing his name with the Canadian government and their super-team Alpha Flight, and also

"OKAY, suckers— you've taken yer BEST SHOT!"

Wolverine clawed and scraped his way through the sewers in order to sneak into the headquarters of the Hellfire Club unnoticed, determined to save his love, Jean Grey.

"Now it's MY turn!"

got a glimpse into his future as an older version of his teammate Kitty Pryde traveled back in time from the days of future past. He was instrumental in defeating the forces of a new incarnation of the Brotherhood of Evil Mutants led by his old flame Mystique, and he faced the horror of the Marauders when this band of evil mutants massacred hundreds of mutants living in the tunnels below Manhattan. Logan opposed the government itself as they imposed registration on his mutant brothers, and battled his own temptations as he fought the Goblyn Queen when New York City became a living inferno.

Uncanny X-Men #141 (Jan. 1981
The Wolverine of a dystopian future, one of the last of the dying mutant race, struggled against the murderous Sentinels.

Uncanny X-Men #227 (Mar.1988
As the government passed strict mutant registration laws Wolverine found more than merely his civil rights in jeopardy.

Uncanny X-Men #251 (Nov. 1989
Crucified by the evil cyborg Reavers in the Australian outback, Wolverine escaped ar agonizing death with the help of Jubilee.

Publication date
January 1987

Editor-in-chief
Jim Shooter

Cover artists
Alan Davis and Paul Neary

Writer
Chris Claremont

Penciller
Alan Davis

Inker
Paul Neary

Colorist
Glynis Oliver

Letterer
Tom Orzechowski

The Uncanny X-Men #213

> "Their rage is matched... by a terrible, transcendent joy— they so love what they do!"

PSYLOCKE ABOUT WOLVERINE AND SABRETOOTH

MAIN CHARACTERS: Psylocke, Rogue, Wolverine, Magneto, Storm, Callisto, Sabretooth
SUPPORTING CHARACTERS: Nightcrawler, Colossus, Kitty Pryde, Lockheed, the New Mutants, Dazzler, Malice, Moira MacTaggart, Sharon Friedlander, Marauders
LOCATIONS: Westchester, New York; Manhattan, New York; Los Angeles, California

Background

In 1986, the comic industry was treated to perhaps its three most important works. Frank Miller's grim and gritty *Batman: The Dark Knight Returns*, Alan Moore and Dave Gibbon's modern parable *Watchmen*, and Art Spiegelman's true tale of the holocaust, *Maus*. One theme all these works had in common was a concern with the dark side of human nature, an examination of the shadows, and the sparks of hope that exist within them both.

Mainstream comics soon began to mirror these themes, their creators fascinated by the sophistication possible in the medium, and inspired to create something of equal maturity. Some succeeded in this goal, while other works merely mimicked the adult levels of brutality and violence found in books like *The Dark Knight Returns*, without the deeper levels of character development and social commentary that made the series what it was.

The X-Men crossover Mutant Massacre was birthed in this brave new environment. It remains one of the bloodiest mutant battles of all time, and the X-Men were caught right in the thick of it.

The Story

After the massacre of the mutant underdwellers known as the Morlocks, Sabretooth finds his way to Xavier's mansion, his bloodlust still unsated...

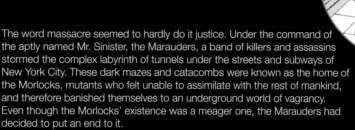

The word massacre seemed to hardly do it justice. Under the command of the aptly named Mr. Sinister, the Marauders, a band of killers and assassins stormed the complex labyrinth of tunnels under the streets and subways of New York City. These dark mazes and catacombs were known as the home of the Morlocks, mutants who felt unable to assimilate with the rest of mankind, and therefore banished themselves to an underground world of vagrancy. Even though the Morlocks' existence was a meager one, the Marauders had decided to put an end to it.

Once in the tunnels, the Marauders started to systematically kill every mutant they came across. Men, women, and children were all the same in the eyes of these merciless killers. The X-Men, X-Factor, and the New Mutants quickly became aware of the situation, and a fierce battle took place beneath the city streets. The mutant heroes finally chased the Marauders away, despite suffering many casualties of their own.

The storm had passed, and now the X-Men were on damage control. While the X-Men's new headmaster, the reformed villain Magneto, searched the Morlock tunnels for signs of life alongside Wolverine, Storm, and the Morlock leader Callisto, the other X-Men recovered in Charles Xavier's mansion in Westchester. Meanwhile mutant powerhouse Rogue, and the telepath Psylocke kept a close watch on the surrounding grounds **(1)**.

As Psylocke, Betsy Braddock was still new to the X-Men's ranks and not an official part of the team. Accordingly, she was anxious to help out her new friends and win their approval. While using the mutant detection system Cerebro, Betsy began to contact the others psychically, hoping she could lend them her assistance **(2)**. Wanting to protect their new friend, the other X-Men turned down her offer, and so Betsy went back to combing the grounds of the X-Men's estate for intruders.

Suddenly, a wave of psychic backlash hit Psylocke so hard, it knocked her from her seat **(3)**. There was an intruder in the grounds. Before Betsy could react, the ruthless mutant Sabretooth barged into her quarters and attacked her. Psylocke barely escaped with her life **(4)**. Though terrified for her own safety, Psylocke led Sabretooth on a chase around the mansion, away from the medical labs that housed her helpless friends, severely injured from the battle with the Marauders in the Morlock tunnels. Her deadly game of tag paid off when she led Sabretooth to Storm's attic room just as Wolverine arrived on the scene.

They'd been down this road before. Fierce enemies and regular sparring partners, Wolverine and Sabretooth began one of their most brutal fights **(5)**. The battle spilled out onto a nearby cliff in the surrounding grounds. Each man took turns ripping and clawing the other, every strike more deadly than the last. However, there was a method in Wolverine's madness. He had been stalling Sabretooth so that Psylocke had time to read the brute's mind and determine who had led the evil Marauders **(6)**. Obtaining the information she needed, Psylocke alerted Wolverine, who admitted his ploy to his opponent. Fearing capture, Sabretooth hurled himself and Wolverine off the cliff and into the river below. Sabretooth disappeared into the murky waters. Though the war was not over, the battle had gone to the heroes, and Psylocke had finally earned her official place in the X-Men team **(7)**.

"Wolverine speaks for us all, Elizabeth. Welcome to the team!"

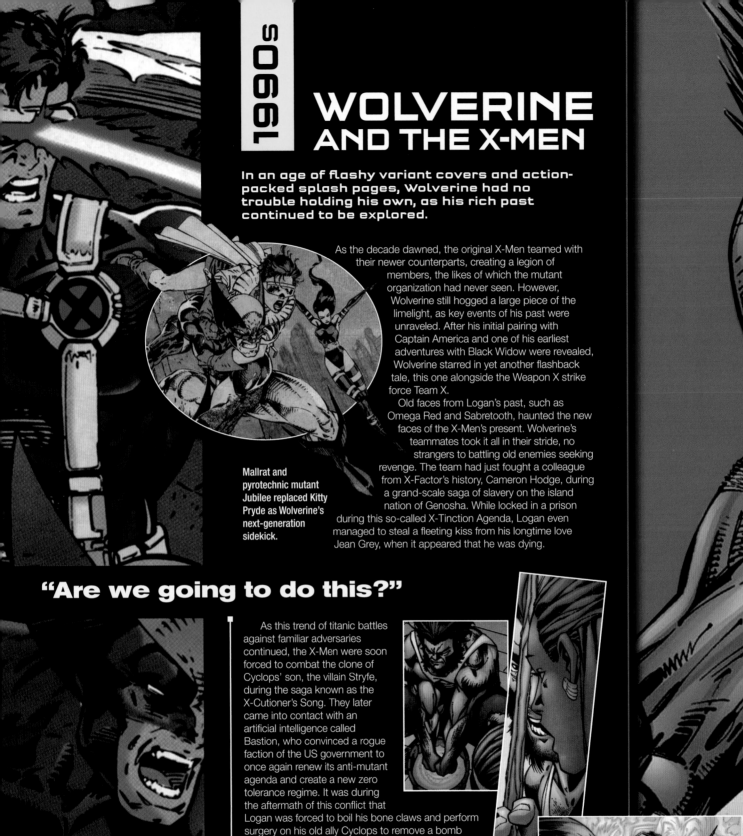

WOLVERINE
AND THE X-MEN

In an age of flashy variant covers and action-packed splash pages, Wolverine had no trouble holding his own, as his rich past continued to be explored.

As the decade dawned, the original X-Men teamed with their newer counterparts, creating a legion of members, the likes of which the mutant organization had never seen. However, Wolverine still hogged a large piece of the limelight, as key events of his past were unraveled. After his initial pairing with Captain America and one of his earliest adventures with Black Widow were revealed, Wolverine starred in yet another flashback tale, this one alongside the Weapon X strike force Team X.

Old faces from Logan's past, such as Omega Red and Sabretooth, haunted the new faces of the X-Men's present. Wolverine's teammates took it all in their stride, no strangers to battling old enemies seeking revenge. The team had just fought a colleague from X-Factor's history, Cameron Hodge, during a grand-scale saga of slavery on the island nation of Genosha. While locked in a prison during this so-called X-Tinction Agenda, Logan even managed to steal a fleeting kiss from his longtime love Jean Grey, when it appeared that he was dying.

Mallrat and pyrotechnic mutant Jubilee replaced Kitty Pryde as Wolverine's next-generation sidekick.

"Are we going to do this?"

As this trend of titanic battles against familiar adversaries continued, the X-Men were soon forced to combat the clone of Cyclops' son, the villain Stryfe, during the saga known as the X-Cutioner's Song. They later came into contact with an artificial intelligence called Bastion, who convinced a rogue faction of the US government to once again renew its anti-mutant agenda and create a new zero tolerance regime. It was during the aftermath of this conflict that Logan was forced to boil his bone claws and perform surgery on his old ally Cyclops to remove a bomb from his friend's chest.

The team subsequently fought the world-devouring Galactus, the shape-changing Skrulls, and the returning threat of Apocalypse. But perhaps their greatest battle of the decade would be against one of their own, when Professor X's dark side manifested as the ultra-powerful entity, Onslaught.

"Not used t'usin' these things fer healin', doc."

The Uncanny X-Men #268
(Sept. 1990)
Wolverine fought against the
Hand both with Black Widow
in the present and with
Captain America in the past.

X-Men #1 (Oct, 1991)
The original X-Men joined
forces with their newer
recruits during a fierce battle
against Magneto.

X-Men #70 (Dec. 1997)
In the wake of the Zero
Tolerance event, the X-Men's
ranks were increased by
several new members.

X-Men #6

> **"Proves a theory o' mine. Maybe Red ain't the only mutant in service of his country?"**

LOGAN AS A MEMBER OF TEAM X

MAIN CHARACTERS: Wolverine, Sabretooth, Psylocke, Omega Red, Maverick, Cyclops, Jubilee, Beast, Gambit, Rogue, Matsu'o Tsurayaba, Dr. Cornelius
SUPPORTING CHARACTERS: Longshot, Lila Cheney, Dazzler, Mojo, Fenris, Birdy, the Hand, Janice Hollenbeck
LOCATIONS: Berlin, Germany; Mojoworld

Publication date
March 1992

Editor-in-chief
Tom DeFalco

Cover artists
Jim Lee and Art Thibert

Writers
Jim Lee and Scott Lobdell

Penciller
Jim Lee

Inker
Art Thibert

Colorist
Joe Rosas

Letterer
Tom Orzechowski

Background

The X-Men had just ventured into uncharted waters. With blockbuster sales on *The Uncanny X-Men* inflated from crossover events like the X-Tinction Agenda storyline, Marvel's premier team of mutants was enjoying a pleasant reinvigoration of its franchise. But Marvel would soon realize that the wave it was riding was of tidal proportions when its all-new monthly ongoing series titled simply *X-Men* was released in October of 1991. Featuring the team's most popular newcomers side by side with the original founding members, longtime writer Chris Claremont alongside superstar artist Jim Lee, as well as five different variant covers, *X-Men* #1 broke all sales records, selling upwards of eight million copies.

Fan favorite scribe Chris Claremont soon left the book after its initial arc, citing creative differences. As writer John Byrne and later Scott Lobdell stepped in to fill the void, they were eased into their transition with plotting help from Jim Lee. To keep audiences glued to their seats, they centered their next landmark story arc around the captivating past of everyone's favorite mutant: Wolverine. In doing so, they continued the title's fast-paced momentum, exemplified by *X-Men* #6.

The Story

While battling a face from his past—Omega Red—Wolverine flashes back to his tenure with Team X and a secret weapon lost to the ravages of time...

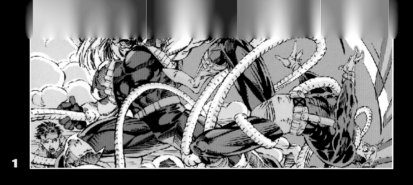

1

2

3

4

The X-Men were just heading out for a pleasant meal. You would think they would realize by now that someone was bound to crash the party. The team was ambushed by Hand ninjas during their trip into town, and Wolverine was shocked to discover his old enemy, Omega Red, working with the devious ninjas. The other X-Men managed to escape thanks to the timely arrival of some of their other teammates, but Logan, the true target of the attack, was captured and brought to a secret hideout in Berlin, Germany. There he was strapped into restraints in front of many of his old foes, including Weapon X's Professor Cornelius, Hand leader Matsu'o Tsurayaba, and the brother and sister team known as Fenris. Planning to probe Wolverine's mind in search of a long-lost innovation called the Carbonadium Synthesizer, the group of villains were interrupted when Logan's old teammate Maverick appeared on the scene. Having worked with Logan during his days with the CIA's covert Team X, Maverick escaped with Wolverine using the X-Men's simultaneous arrival as cover. While Cyclops and the others became locked in battle with Omega Red and his life-draining "mutant death factor" **(1)**, Maverick injected Wolverine with a large dose of neuroapinephrine in order to revive his injured friend **(2)**.

But this team of core X-Men wasn't the only band of heroes finding themselves in strange surroundings. In a dimension knows as Mojoworld, Longshot, Dazzler, and Lila Cheney were facing a dire threat of their own, the TV-obsessed villain Mojo himself **(3)**. While these heroes found refuge with that world's rebel forces, back in Berlin, as Logan's body began to heal from the injuries inflicted in Dr. Cornelius's lab, Logan's mind traveled back more than thirty years to his days with Team X **(4)**. On a mission to sabotage a Russian super-soldier program and rescue the double agent Janice Hollenbeck, Logan, along with teammates Maverick and Sabretooth, accidentally angered the Russians' very own super-soldier, Omega Red. Attempting to escape, but facing a ten-story drop, Sabretooth decided to kill Hollenbeck, calling the woman a liability. As Omega Red closed in on the team, the trio leapt from the building. They hit the pavement below, but somehow survived the impact. It was only then that Logan's suspicions were confirmed: all three of the Team X members were mutants.

After their mission, during debriefing, the team admitted that they had failed to bring back the Carbonadium Synthesizer. In reality, Logan had hidden it inside the dead body of Janice Hollenbeck; he no longer trusted his Team X colleagues and didn't want the weapon to fall into the wrong hands. The mission was nevertheless regarded as a success. The trio had prevented the development of Omega Red and caused the Russians to put the villain in suspended animation. However, Logan was still angered at Sabretooth's killing of Janice Hollenbeck, the innocent double agent, and in a fit of anger resigned from Team X **(5)**.

Back in the present, Wolverine finally awoke from his sleep, and despite not recognizing Maverick, teamed up with his old friend in order to battle Sabretooth **(6)**, who had arrived on the scene as a hired gun for Matsu'o Tsurayaba. With the help of the brainwashed Psylocke, Sabretooth overpowered Wolverine and Maverick, kidnapping them and delivering them to his bosses **(7)**.

The action continued into the final issue of the arc. Wolverine and the rest of the X-Men taken captive by Omega Red escaped their bonds with the aid of Psylocke who had been pretending to be dead. Back at full strength, the team rallied to defeat Matsu'o and his partners, and retrieved the C-Synthesizer from Janice Hollenbeck's grave, giving the important device to Maverick for safekeeping.

5

6

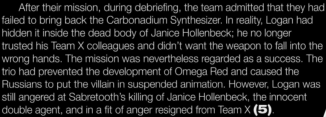

7

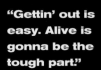

"Gettin' out is easy. Alive is gonna be the tough part."

WOLVERINE
AND THE X-MEN

A cultural icon in the present day, Wolverine has quickly become the most famous of the X-Men and a dedicated and loyal member of the team.

The decade began with the X-Men in the same state of convoluted organization as at the end of the 1990s. However, the team soon received a facelift and complete restructuring. Xavier's Institute once again became a place of learning, its focus switching from being simply an X-Men complex to a school once again, one that would train the next generation of mutants for the roles that awaited them. With a core group of so-called New X-Men on the teaching roster, including Professor X, Wolverine, Cyclops, Jean Grey, Beast, and even Emma Frost, the White Queen, the mutant children of the world flocked to this safe haven, especially when Professor X publicly announced that he was a mutant.

Despite their newfound passion as professors of mutant studies, the X-Men nevertheless found time to save the planet on a few occasions. During this era, the X-Men faced the likes of Professor X's evil twin Cassandra Nova, the disturbed turncoat Xorn, and even a few renegade students. Meanwhile, Wolverine learned a bit more about the scope of the Weapon X project, and once again lost his love Jean Grey. She was killed by Xorn, when the powerful mutant came to believe the delusion that he in fact was Magneto.

As more changes rocked the X-Men's universe, including a permanent move to California, the group's roster altered a few times, yet the faithful Wolverine always remained a constant.

Kitty Pryde and the recently resurrected Colossus would later join the X-Men's core team.

"I remember... my whole life."

When the Scarlet Witch returned the world to the way it had been, she used her chaos magic to reduce the number of mutants to 198. Wolverine still remembered all of his past that he had recalled during the House of M saga. Now Logan was awake in his world, remembering everything.

"Everything."

Astonishing X-Men #1
(July 2004)
As Xavier's school reopened for business, Wolverine and Cyclops had it out, both grieving over Jean Grey's recent death.

Uncanny X-Men #500
(September 2008)
The X-Men set up their new digs in San Francisco, alongside old friends Angel, Storm, and Nightcrawler.

X-Men: Deadly Genesis #1
(January 2006)
The team discovered that Professor X had led a secret group of X-Men years ago, one that didn't survive past its first mission.

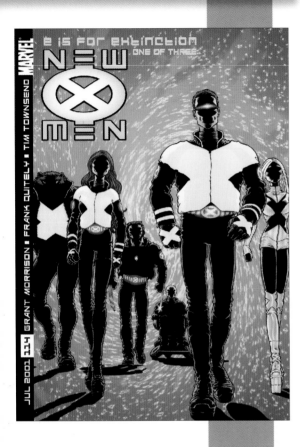

Publication date
July 2001

Editor-in-chief
Joe Quesada

Cover Artist
Frank Quitely

Writer
Grant Morrison

Penciller
Frank Quitely

Inker
Tim Townsend

Colorist
Brian Haberlin

Letterer
Comicraft

New
X-Men
#114

"Forget your dental practice, Mr. Trask. Your future lies in genocide!"

CASSANDRA NOVA TO A CAPTIVE DONALD TRASK)

MAIN CHARACTERS: Beast, Jean Grey, Wolverine, Professor X, Cyclops, White Queen, Cassandra Nova
SUPPORTING CHARACTERS: Ugly John, Donald Trask
LOCATIONS: Westchester, New York; Sydney, Australia; Ecuadorian jungle

Background

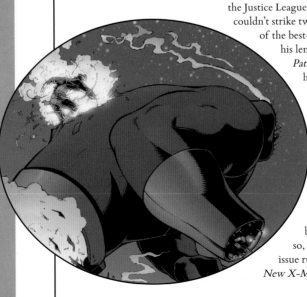

Renowned writer Grant Morrison had already done wonders for the Justice League, and there was no indication that lightning couldn't strike twice. Morrison had spent his career crafting some of the best-received works of comic book fiction, including his lengthy runs on both *Animal Man* and *Doom Patrol* for DC/Vertigo. In the late 1990s, Morrison had turned his efforts toward relaunching DC's flagship team, the Justice League, in a series entitled *JLA*. Morrison had an instant hit on his hands, and so it was only natural that Marvel would seek out his talents.

Alongside brilliant artist Frank Quitely, Morrison brought the X-Men back to their schoolyard roots, granting the title a new name, and ignoring much of the confusing history that had amassed during the heroes' lengthy lifetimes. Morrison only included the best and the brightest of the team and, in doing so, created a sensation throughout his forty-plus issue run on the title, which began with his debut on *New X-Men* #114.

The Story

While the X-Men restructure their organization, a new villain named Cassandra Nova sets a horrifying plan in motion with the intention of destroying all mutants...

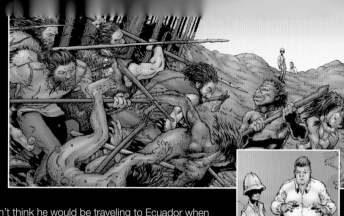

Donald Trask didn't think he would be traveling to Ecuador when he woke up that morning. A moderately successful dentist in Albuquerque, Trask led a pretty normal life, so he was astonished when a woman named Cassandra Nova whisked him away in a helicopter, convincing him that she was a government agent, and that he was needed to perform a black ops root canal on the President of the United States. Not wanting to rock the boat, Trask left with this mysterious woman. The next thing he knew, he was hooked up to a virtual reality machine, landing in the jungles of Ecuador.

As his host, Cassandra Nova, narrated, Trask witnessed a race of *Homo sapiens sapien* wipe out their ancestors, *Homo sapiens neanderthalensis* **(1)**. The bloody display was too much for him. Trask removed his virtual reality helmet just as his helicopter touched down.

Meanwhile, back in Westchester, New York, Jean Grey and Beast were busy helping Professor X try out the new Cerebra machine **(2)**, a more powerful version of their Cerebro mutant detection system. Despite having trouble fine-tuning the device owing to his recent second mutation, Beast managed to get Cerebra up and running. Xavier began an informal meeting with his two companions on the psychic plane, as well as with Wolverine and Cyclops, who happened to be piloting one of the school's new X-Wing jets home from Australia at the time. After the team had discussed their new responsibilities at the school, as well as their new leather uniforms, Professor X requested that Cyclops and Wolverine check out a powerful mutant spike that he had detected with Cerebra's help. This mutant beacon just happened to be coming from Ecuador.

Professor X concluded the meeting, and the other X-Men went about their business. Just as Professor X was ending his session with Cerebra, he felt a mysterious presence attempting to take over his mind. He only survived this attack with the help of Jean Grey **(3)**, and by threatening to shoot himself in the head then and there. As the presence abandoned his mind, Professor X realized the danger he had sent his X-Men toward. Cyclops and Wolverine were heading straight toward that very same powerful mutant mind.

Meanwhile, back in the jungle, Cassandra Nova was leading her guest through thick foliage until she finally arrived at her destination: the Master Mold **(4)**. A leftover factory producing wild, self-replicating mutant-hunting Sentinels, the Master Mold was created by Donald Trask's ancestor, Bolivar Trask. As Cassandra Nova allowed a group of men to be slaughtered in order to make her point **(5)**, she revealed to Donald that only his voice could command the wild machines. She needed Donald's help to destroy the mutant populace of the world, and he could do so by merely uttering a few simple words that would bring the sleeping Master Mold to life **(6)**.

In later issues, despite the X-Men finally bringing Cassandra Nova to justice, the twisted villain still managed the single greatest atrocity in the history of mutantkind with the help of Trask's wild Sentinels—the destruction of the entire mutant island nation of Genosha.

"Oh have a guess, Mr. Trask. Don't make me point to it."

CHAPTER **FOUR**

Wolverine Alone

1ST SOLO SERIES

Wolverine was ready for his close-up. Though his tenure with the X-Men was quite short compared to that of the team's original founding members, Logan quickly became the title's favorite son. Readers everywhere were captivated by the character's mysterious history and unwavering code of honor, so fan favorite writer and *X-Men* scribe Chris Claremont teamed with legendary *Daredevil* artist Frank Miller to give the feral mutant his first four-issue miniseries.

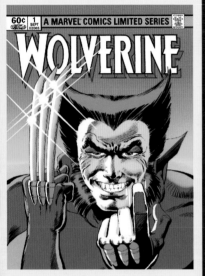

Wolverine #1, September 1982
An instant hit, Wolverine's first limited series captured the true essence of the character, complete with hard-boiled narration, fast-paced action, and even a bit of romance.

WOLVERINE DEPARTS

When Logan found a stack of his letters to girlfriend Mariko Yashida returned to his address, he hopped the next fight to Japan to check on his long-distance love. There he was met by an old friend and former intelligence agent, Asano Kimura.

MARIKO'S HUSBAND

Informed by his old friend that his lover had taken a husband, Wolverine set out to confront Mariko, only to discover that she was trapped in an abusive marriage to Noburo-Hideki, arranged by her father, the corrupt martial arts master, Lord Shingen.

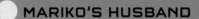

"He deserves it. He beats you, Mariko. If I don't stop him, he'll keep doing it!"

FIGHTING LORD SHINGEN

Challenging Logan to a duel with wooden practice swords, Shingen aimed his attacks perfectly, striking Wolverine's pain centers in order to provoke him into popping his claws. As her father hoped, Mariko was appalled and decided that she wanted nothing more to do with Logan.

THE HAND ATTACKS!

Alone and defeated, Wolverine was discovered by the mysterious Yukio, a lone warrior who was secretly in Shingen's employ. On the run from the Hand, Yukio and Logan had a brief romantic encounter before he discovered her true dark allegiances.

BETRAYED

Despite Yukio revealing her true love to Wolverine, her betrayal was too much for the feral mutant, and he attacked her. Yukio was saved from Logan's wrath by the timely intervention of the Hand's forces, and she and Wolverine would meet again later, as Logan was storming Shingen's home. Killing Mariko's husband, Yukio ultimately won back Wolverine's favor before disappearing into the night.

"You'd better kill me now, Yukio. You won't get a second chance."

Wolverine

DEATH OF SHINGEN?

When Mariko became aware of her father's criminal ties, Logan was able to confront Lord Shingen without fear of her disapproval. After a fierce duel, Wolverine managed to run Shingen through, and soon after, he and Mariko became engaged.

SNIKT

2ND SOLO SERIES

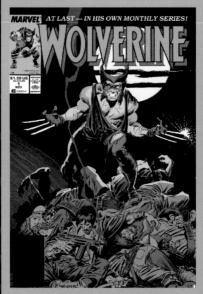

Wolverine #1, November 1988
After Marvel had tested the waters with a ten-part Wolverine story in the anthology title *Marvel Comics Presents*, Logan's very own series debuted with great fanfare.

"Some people don't deserve to die easy."

Wolverine

After the success of his first solo series and his continued popularity in *The Uncanny X-Men*, Marvel was finally cutting Wolverine loose. Logan was given another chance at solo stardom, this time chronicled by the initial creative team of writer Chris Claremont and artist John Buscema. Wolverine was once again the star of his own title, and at last it was an ongoing series.

MADRIPOOR

Taking a break from his adventures with the X-Men, Logan journeyed to his home away from home—the corrupt Asian isle known as Madripoor. Operating out of the Princess Bar and teaming with allies such as Jessica Drew and Tyger Tiger, Logan took up the identity of Patch, and fought the likes of Bloodsport, Roughouse, and the Silver Samurai.

SABRETOOTH

When Victor Creed, aka Sabretooth, seemingly killed Logan's true love, Silver Fox, he started a bloody feud that would run the course of both mutants' lives. Sabretooth returned many times to plague Wolverine—at one point even claiming to be the hero's father.

WITHOUT ADAMANTIUM

In a fierce battle alongside his fellow X-Men, Logan had the adamantium covering his bones literally ripped out of his body by the master of magnetism, Magneto. After barely surviving the event, Logan was forced to rely on his natural bone claws for the dozens of adventures that followed.

COSTUME CHANGE

After returning to the headquarters of the Weapon X program and becoming frustrated when he attempted to recall his past memories, Wolverine decided a change was in order, and switched back to his original yellow and blue duds.

SPANISH CIVIL WAR

When reminiscing about the past with his former Alpha Flight ally Puck, Wolverine found himself and his old friend sucked into a time warp when the evil Lady Deathstrike tried to abuse the mutant Gateway's powers. Traveling back to Spain in the year 1937, Wolverine relived his time with writer Ernest Hemingway in Guernica during the Spanish Civil War. Crossing paths with his old female foe just as the time vortex caught up with both of them, Deathstrike and Logan fought through time to arrive safely back in the present.

> "I'll never be an animal again! I'm Logan! I'm human!."
> Wolverine

> "...get outta my face... and leave a man to his dirty business."
> Wolverine

ELSIE-DEE AND ALBERT

Created by Donald Pierce, the leader of the cyborg gang known as the Reavers, the android Elsie-Dee and the robot Wolverine known as Albert were specifically designed to kill the real flesh-and-blood version of Logan. However, after Wolverine saved Elsie from self-destructing when she confronted him at Venice Beach, both cyborgs rejected their programming and became Logan's allies.

NOT THE END

In the final adventure of his first ongoing title, Wolverine helped an alcoholic internal affairs detective named Lester Brown take down corrupt cop Scott McLawry. To prove the cop was a murderer, Logan tricked McLawry into shooting him and then leading him to his burial site, where McLawry tried to hide Wolverine's supposedly dead body.

3RD SOLO SERIES

It was time for Wolverine to once again make his snikt heard. Debuting only a single month after his first ongoing series ended, Wolverine's second monthly effort kicked off with the first-string talent of writer Greg Rucka and artist Darick Robertson. Logan's new series proved a hit with the readers, climbing in popularity when other talents like Mark Millar, John Romita Jr., and Jeph Loeb joined the title's rotating creative cast.

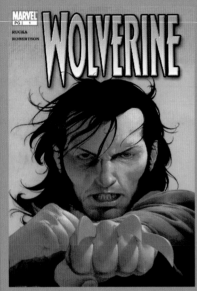

***Wolverine* #1, July 2003**
Featuring a cover painting by Esad Ribic, the first issue of Wolverine's current series pitted Logan against more down to Earth violence rather than super-powered foes.

THE DEATH OF LUCY BRADDOCK

Logan made the acquaintance of shy waitress Lucy Braddock at a small roadside diner, but he was later appalled to discover the girl that had befriended him dead in her apartment. Following her murderer's trail back to a bizarre cult known as the Brothers, Logan set free the criminals' captive women and killed their leader, the would-be messiah known only as Cry.

Even if you do nothing more please, do this for me.

ENEMY OF THE STATE

Brainwashed in a combined effort by the criminal organizations Hydra and the Hand, Logan became a wanted man as he did the bidding of his new masters—attacking his former allies the Fantastic Four, Daredevil, Elektra, and at one point even storming the X-Men's mansion.

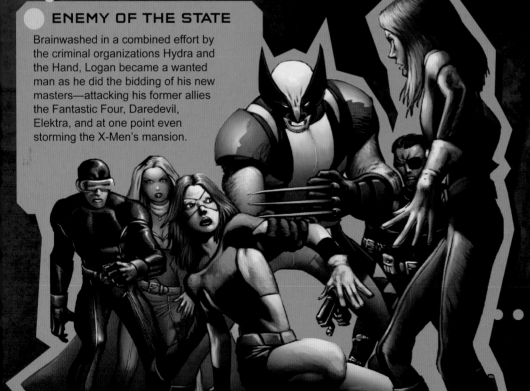

AGENT CASSIE LATHROP

While on the hunt for Lucy Braddock's killer, Wolverine attracted the attention of Cassie Lathrop, a government agent from the department of alcohol, tobacco, and firearms. Lathrop became obsessed with the feral mutant after he saved her life, and they later embarked on a brief romance.

DEPARTMENT K REVISITED

When Wolverine and his fellow heroes stopped the Scarlet Witch from shaping the world to suit her own needs in the alternate House of M reality, Wolverine found that all of his memories were returned to him. Now armed with a long list of those who wronged him in the past, Logan headed to the old Weapon X complex to discover a hidden truth.

HEART ATTACKS

After witnessing the death of his long lost love known as the Native, and then seeing his newly discovered flame named Amir die before his eyes, Logan seemed finished with matters of the heart. He proved the point when he tracked down his old lover and enemy Mystique, and showed his prey no mercy.

> "I might hate myself in the morning... but I'm going to enjoy this."
>
> Wolverine

SABRETOOTH

During his final duel with Sabretooth, Wolverine learned that more than lifelong animosity connected him to his brutish opponent. He discovered that the two were inextricably linked as members of a subset of mutantkind known as the Lupine.

The beautiful Mariko caught Logan's attention right away, and their tumultuous relationship lasted for years.

It was instant attraction. If only they could have left it at that. Mariko Yashida was near royalty, the leader of Japan's Yashida Clan, a powerful family with a storied history and ties into the Yakuza, Japan's version of the mafia. Despite her corrupt connections, Wolverine still found himself falling for Mariko's traditional beauty and grace. The two formed a long distance relationship that was interrupted when Mariko's father, Lord Shingen, reemerged in her life after a mysterious absence. Shingen forced his daughter to marry the abusive Noburu-Hideki, one of his associates, to maintain the family honor, thus placing a permanent roadblock between the two lovers.

FIRST APPEARANCE
Uncanny X-Men #118

OCCUPATION Former head of ancestral Japanese clan

BASE Ancestral Seat of Clan Yashida, Miyago Prefecture, Japan

AFFILIATIONS Clan Yashida

RELATIVES Lord Shingen (father), Silver Samurai (half brother), Sunfire (cousin)

POWERS/WEAPONS None

Mariko's close ties to the Yakuza have frequently put her in harm's way, from the threats of her jealous half brother, the criminal Silver Samurai, to the menace of the clandestine ninja group, the Hand.

Mariko was one of the few women who could tame Logan, reducing the savage beast to a lovesick puppy.

MARIKO YASHIDA

MARRIAGE MISERY

Mariko's first marriage proved to be short-lived. After the corrupt Shingen fell in battle to Wolverine, her husband, Noburu-Hideki, died at the hands of Wolverine's ally Yukio. Mariko was finally free to give her hand to Logan. They were soon engaged, and they organized a small, traditional ceremony with the X-Men as guests of honor. But when Mariko fell under the mind-controlling powers of Jason Wyngarde, the mutant villain also known as Mastermind, she left Logan at the altar, breaking his heart and crushing his spirit.

MURDER!

Once Mariko regained her senses, she realized her mistake. However, the shame of her family's criminal history weighed heavily on her conscience, and she vowed that before she and Logan could marry, she must first mend her family's ways and sever all of their illegitimate ties. Later, during a return trip to Japan, Wolverine came into conflict with a faction of ninja assassins from the Hand led by Matsu'o Tsurayaba. Matsu'o was planning a hostile takeover of the Yashida Clan, and, out of nowhere, offered Mariko a permanent peace agreement between the Hand and the Yashida Clan. All Mariko had to do was remove one of her own fingers with Tsurayaba's blade, an act of respect for the dishonor her house had caused his. Complying with Matsu'o's wishes, Mariko began to cut off her pinky finger, realizing too late that the blade was spiked with fatal blowfish poison.

EXILES

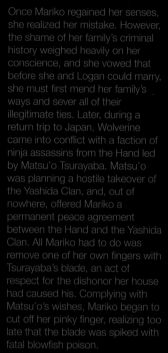

Outside the Marvel Universe proper, a group of adventurers exist, traveling from one dimension to another, in order to mend ripples in various continuities. The Mariko Yashida from another universe was a onetime member of this band of Exiles. This version of Mariko called herself Sunfire and possessed solar-based mutant abilities.

VOW OF REVENGE

As she lay dying in Logan's arms from the fatal toxin, Mariko revealed that she had finally severed her criminal ties and the two were now free to wed. This tragic irony made Logan's grief even harder to bear. With the pain proving too much for her, Mariko begged Logan to end her life quickly. Logan grudgingly granted her this last request, running her through with his claws. With his heart full of rage, he swore to visit Matsu'o, Mariko's killer, every year at midnight on the anniversary of her death and slice off one of his body parts.

CHAPTER FIVE

The Further Adventures of Wolverine

"WHAT HAVE I DONE?!"

Hers is a case of twisted honor, the result of a demented mind searching to make reparation for past wrongs. When Yuriko Oyama first entered Wolverine's life, she was a woman cursed to bear a scar of shame upon her face from the failures of her father, Lord Dark Wind. Dark Wind had been a kamikaze pilot during the Japanese attack on Pearl Harbor, but had failed to die for his cause, merely suffering horrible scarring. After spending time as a shamed prisoner of war, he went on to develop a process for bonding bone with the unbreakable alloy adamantium. The formula was later stolen from him. Ashamed of his failings, Dark Wind had branded his daughter's face with his mark, fueling her hatred for him. Finally Yuriko could contain her anger no longer and she slew her father. She later regretted her rash actions and, determined to make amends, donned samurai garb and changed her name to Lady Deathstrike, vowing to seek out all those who had benefited from Dark Wind's lost technology.

One of the first on Deathstrike's list was Wolverine. Despite Logan having had no say in the adamantium addition to his skeleton, Deathstrike grew to hate the mutant, especially after being easily defeated by Wolverine and his allies on their first encounter. Her hatred soon developed into an obsession. Deathstrike paid a visit to the mad science lab known as the Body Shop, in order to have her body augmented by the superhuman Spiral and become a living weapon. There, she was put through a biomed transmutation to become a cybernetic organism, more machine than woman, with unbreakable bones and claws able to slice through virtually anything.

Despite her demonic appearance, Lady Deathstrike maintains an unswerving code of honor. Though she is ruthless and will kill without feeling, she wishes to give Wolverine a warrior's death, and has passed up opportunities to murder the mutant when he was unprepared for her attack.

After a long operation and a dip in a nutrient bath, Deathstrike was reborn.

FIRST APPEARANCE
Daredevil #197

REAL NAME *Yuriko Oyama*

OCCUPATION *Assassin, CEO of Oyama Heavy Industries*

BASE *Mobile*

AFFILIATIONS Reavers, Thunderbolts

POWERS/WEAPONS
Adamantium fingertip claws. Self-repairing, enhanced cyborg body. Martial arts expert. Adamantium-laced unbreakable skeleton.

LADY
DEATHSTRIKE

THE TRUE AND ULTIMATE WOMAN OF WAR

"Of we two—only the best shall survive!"

Wounded Wolf

It was the holiday season, and Lady Deathstrike was ready to give Wolverine her lethal gift. Armed with her newly upgraded cyborg body, Deathstrike attacked Logan, their fierce battle reducing Wolverine to his feral, primitive state. As shoppers bustled through Manhattan's South Street Seaport, wary of the quickly accumulating snow, Katie Power, the child hero known as Energizer, stumbled upon Wolverine, as he was being chased by Deathstrike's cyborg Reaver companions. Katie helped her old acquaintance hide from his hunters until he regained his human sensibilities. The falling snow rapidly gave way to a blizzard, giving Wolverine the perfect cover to make quick work of Deathstrike's Reaver henchmen. The scene was set for a final showdown between Wolverine and Lady Deathstrike. The two warriors scratched and clawed at each other until experience won out, and Yuriko was left a helpless pile of flesh and machinery, begging for death. This Logan refused to grant her, finding her current plight much more fitting to her crimes.

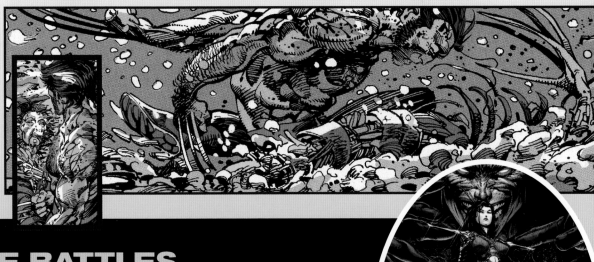

THE BATTLES

Just like the mad woman herself, Lady Deathstrike's hatred refused to die. She later returned to help Donald Pierce and his cyborg Reavers crucify Logan in the Australian outback. However, on that occasion Deathstrike refused to kill her opponent, wanting to defeat him in a fair fight. Still later, she journeyed into the past to hunt Logan during the Spanish Civil War. Most recently, Deathstrike teamed with the mutant-hating Purifiers. This time she wasn't even granted the opportunity to battle Wolverine, as Logan sicced X-23, the young clone of himself, on the warrior woman. This slight only increased Deathstrike's hatred towards her archenemy.

SAVAGE LAND

Jungle Adventure

Wolverine wasn't much for theater. After all, his life provided him with more than enough drama. But when spending a rare evening out at a Broadway play, Logan got into a fight with a cyborg that hailed from the Savage Land. Wolverine headed to this land, where he found his home with a primitive tribe. While there, he formed an intimate relationship with the clan's female leader, Gahck. He soon realized that his presence was a result of the manipulations of the evil Apocalypse. Battling the overlord only to discover that he was merely an android of the villainous mutant, Wolverine fled the Savage Land, leaving behind Gahck, who was pregnant with a child that may well be his.

It is a land untouched by time. A primitive ecosystem preserved from the ravages of civilized man by its hidden location on the continent of Antarctica. Home not only to tribes of prehistoric men and animals, the Savage Land has also served as a refuge for many a mutant seeking an escape from the modern world.

Sauron Battles Wolverine

Karl Lykos, the alter ego of the corrupt Sauron, has often called the Savage Land home, the primeval landscape proving to be a natural home for his pterodactyl-like alter ego that feeds off the life forces of others. His schemes have attracted Wolverine to this land many times, and Sauron has proven no match for the feral mutant, despite having home advantage. In a recent clash, Sauron led not only Wolverine to his doorstep, but also the New Avengers, who were seeking justice for a prison breakout at the Raft penitentiary in Manhattan that Sauron had been party to.

call of the wild

The tropical environment of the Savage Land is filled with active volcanoes and wildlife thought extinct for millennia. It was created by a god-like race of beings called the Beyonders as a hunting ground. Rich in the rare mineral vibranium, the Savage Land has often attracted unwanted attention, including recent mining by a corrupt faction of the government agency SHIELD.

Wolverine and his X-Men allies have had a long history with the Savage Land. On one early voyage there, Magneto used the land as a hideout, transforming the primitive people into his mutates. On a more recent adventure, Wolverine and the New Avengers discovered a crashed Skrull spaceship in the Savage Land's Jurassic jungles. The craft contained Skrull versions of many of the X-Men of the past.

His only religion is his belief in the survival of the fittest. He is one of the oldest known mutants, and before he is through, he will see himself become a god.

APOCALYPSE

FIRST APPEARANCE
Marvel Graphic Novels #17

REAL NAME *En Sabah Nur*

OCCUPATION *Conqueror*

AFFILIATIONS *Leader of the Alliance of Evil, Horsemen of Apocalypse, Dark Riders*

POWERS/WEAPONS *Molecular control over body enables shape changing, teleporting, energy projection, and absorption. Flight. Superstrength.*

DARK ORIGINS
The boy who would become Apocalypse was abandoned in the deserts of Egypt, his rightful parents frightened by his gray skin. He was taken in by a band of nomads, and named En Sabah Nur ("The First One"). Captured and enslaved by King Ozymandias, Nur discovered advanced technology hidden in Ozymandias's ancient kingdom. Nur soon rose to power, preserving Ozymandias as his aid, and forcing the once powerful king to chronicle the every move of Nur's new alias: Apocalypse.

MUTANT OVERLORD
As the modern era dawned, Apocalypse became obsessed with thinning the Earth's population, believing from his own personal struggles that only the strong should survive. Convinced he was the first mutant, Apocalypse naturally became interested in powerful mutant groups such as the X-Men, first challenging the heroes of X-Factor with his handpicked powerhouses, the Alliance of Evil.

MEETING WOLVERINE
Apocalypse wished to test the abilities of Wolverine. When one of Nur's robot duplicates began to overstep his duties, Apocalypse manipulated Logan into traveling to the Savage Land and destroying the android for him. Satisfied that Wolverine had passed the test, Apocalypse appeared to the feral mutant in hologram form, as if to foreshadow some corrupt future partnership between the two.

HORSEMEN

After gathering a few incarnations of his augmented followers, the Horsemen, Apocalypse set his sights once again on Wolverine, arranging for the mutant's capture by his alien Skrull allies. Forcing Logan through a painful adamantium bonding process as well as reconditioning his mind, Apocalypse transformed Logan into the perfect killing machine called Death, before Wolverine's strong will finally prevailed.

Over the years, En Sabah Nur has returned to plague the X-Men time and time again. He transformed many of their roster and friends into his Horsemen, including Archangel, Sunfire, Caliban, Polaris, and Gambit.

Weapon X #1

Publication date
March 1995

Editor-in-chief
Bob Harras

Cover artist
Adam Kubert

Writer
Larry Hama

Breakdowns
Adam Kubert

Finishes
Karl Kesel, Dan Green, Chris Warner

Colorist
Mike Thomas

Letterer
Pat Brosseau

"—There's somethin' lurkin' in the dark here...

...and it ain't a pretty sight!"

WEAPON X

MAIN CHARACTERS: Jean Grey, Weapon X, Havok, Apocalypse, Cyclops
SUPPORTING CHARACTERS: Androids of the Sensor Control Center, Dark Beast, Abyss, Holocaust, Bolivar Trask, Moira Trask, Emma Frost, Mariko Yashida, Brian Braddock, Magma
LOCATIONS: Great Sea Wall, Atlantic Ocean; Apocalypse's Citadel, New York City, New York; London, England

Background

Marvel had stopped publishing *Wolverine*—for four months at least. As Marvel started to realize the lucrative benefits of tie-ins and crossover events, they decided it was time to shake up the X-Men universe. Enter *X-Men: Alpha*, a one-shot special that placed the entire mutant cast, as well as a few other familiar Marvel faces, into the nightmare alternate reality of a world conquered by the powerful evil mutant Apocalypse. In this dystopian vision of the Marvel Universe, the X-Men's founder, Professor Charles Xavier, had died years earlier, altering the landscape of mutantkind. The result was a world in which a reformed Magneto led the X-Men, Apocalypse ruled North America with an iron fist, and what few humans still lived had created a resistance based in London, England.

In order to accommodate this massive story arc, Marvel changed the name of all the titles in the X-Men line of comics, in order to reflect this brave new world. Wolverine's title was temporarily replaced for four issues with *Weapon X*, starring Logan and Jean Grey, raising sales on the comic and proving this Age of Apocalypse stunt a huge success.

The Story

Trapped in a world where Apocalypse rules all, lovers Logan and Jean Grey must decide how far they're willing to go to taste true freedom...

1

2

6

It was supposed to be a simple favor for the Human High Council. This was a rare feat in itself, as Logan rarely did favors for anyone, let alone a ragtag group of human rebels fighting an impossible war against the all-powerful mutant overlord Apocalypse. These days Logan was a mercenary called Weapon X, and along with his lover and partner, Jean Grey, was only interested in looking out for his own interests. And he'd paid dearly for those interests, including the loss of his left hand to his archenemy— Apocalypse's loyal lapdog, Scott Summers.

Regardless of his image, Logan still had a bigger heart than he let on, especially when it came to Jean. Before he knew it, he and Jean were riding the back of a giant Sentinel, storming Apocalypse's Great Sea Wall. As Logan headed deeper into the base, Jean Grey was attacked by Prelate Havok, another of Apocalypse's loyal mutant servants (1). After Weapon X accomplished his mission, destroying a few computer consoles and effectively creating a hole in Apocalypse's defenses of North America (2), Logan returned to help Jean defeat Havok (3). With their mission complete, Logan and Jean hitched a ride on their Sentinel and returned to London, England, the headquarters of the human resistance (4).

3

Back in the New York City citadel of Apocalypse, Prelate Scott Summers and Apocalypse himself were informed of this most recent attack on their property (5). As Apocalypse pondered what exactly Logan and Jean were doing during this seemingly incidental raid (6), back in London's Big Ben tower, the Human High Council found themselves under attack by the mutant Magma (7). As Weapon X made short work of the fiery attacker, the Council's leader, Brian Braddock made up his mind (8). He gave the go ahead for Project Scorched Earth, a plan to drop a barrage of nuclear bombs on North America.

"How convenient to find the central committee all set up like ducks in a row!"

As the series continued, Logan and Jean began to drift apart, finding themselves on different sides of the rather important issue of bombing Apocalypse's home. Jean wanted an end to the evil mutant's reign but she couldn't justify all the innocent North Americans that would die in the attack as well. Logan simply wanted an end to the age of Apocalypse, no matter how drastic the measure. This divide soon proved too much for Jean, and she abandoned Logan, heading back to the United States in order to warn them of the coming Armageddon. Knowing Jean was about to sabotage the only hope for human/mutant coexistence, and freedom from the enslavement of Apocalypse, Weapon X still could not bring himself to do what needed to be done and end Jean's life. Instead, he simply kissed her goodbye and let her leave, knowing he would probably never see his lover's face again.

7

As Jean Grey reunited with her old flame Scott Summers, managing to convert the Prelate to her anti-Apocalypse agenda, Weapon X convinced the mutant known as Gateway to enlist his teleportation abilities for the betterment of the world, bringing the reluctant mutant back with him to England. Soon Logan was at the helm of the human's invasion, leading an armada of flying fortresses toward North America, only to discover that Brian Braddock, the leader of the resistance, was in fact a traitor in league with Apocalypse. As Magneto's X-Men simultaneously waged a final surge on Apocalypse's stronghold in New York—now with the aid of Jean Grey and Scott Summers—Logan and his crew defeated Braddock, and through the use of Gateway's teleportation portal, arrived at Apocalypse's citadel with their nuclear payload in tow. While Magneto literally ripped Apocalypse in two during a climactic final battle, the bombs began to fall. And just like that, the age of Apocalypse ended in a flash of pure white light.

4

5

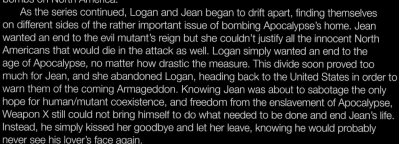

8

REVENGE!

"WE ARE ALL BUT BIT PLAYERS IN A TRAGEDY FAR LARGER THAN ANY OF US...

A TRAGEDY CALLED LIFE, LOGAN."

MAGNETO

LOSING HIS EDGE

In a bloody battle between Magneto and the X-Men on the villain's space satellite Avalon, Wolverine managed to get close enough to Magneto to cut an X into his chest with his claws. Magneto mustered all his magnetic powers in a brutal strike against Wolverine, literally pulling at the very adamantium that was bonded to Wolverine's bones. He ripped the metal out of Wolverine's body and through his skin in large liquid clumps, putting Logan into a state of shock from which he barely recovered even as his teammates evacuated him back to Earth. Slowly recuperating, Wolverine soon realized that his life would never again be the same. When he finally gained the strength to pop his claws, all that emerged from his fists were jagged bones, a mere skeleton of the weapons he used to rely upon.

WOLVERINE #75

> " **"I may be down, but I ain't out ...and I'm still the best at what I do!"**

WOLVERINE

MAIN CHARACTERS: Wolverine, Professor X, Jean Grey, Rogue, Quicksilver, Bishop, Moira MacTaggert, Jubilee, Gambit, Psylocke, Kitty Pryde, Cyclops, Storm, Beast
SUPPORTING CHARACTERS: Sabretooth, various Team X members, Lady Deathstrike, Magneto, Carol Hines, Dr. Abraham Cornelius, Illyana Rasputin
LOCATIONS: Space entering Earth's orbit; dream plane; Xavier Institute, Westchester, New York

Publication date
November, 1993

Editor-in-chief
Tom DeFalco

Cover artists
Adam Kubert and Mark Farmer

Writer
Larry Hama

Penciller
Adam Kubert

Inker
Mark Farmer, Dan Green, Mark Pennington

Colorist
Steve Buccellato

Letterer
Pat Brosseau

Background

The X-Men were turning thirty, and the years were about to take their toll on Wolverine. In order to boost sales as well as celebrate three decades of the world's favorite mutants, Marvel decided to enhance all six of the main X-Men titles (*The Uncanny X-Men, X-Men, X-Factor, X-Force, Excalibur,* and *Wolverine*) with extra pages and cardstock covers, each topped with a hologram sticker. To make the event even more enticing, an epic story called "Fatal Attractions" was concocted by writers Fabian Nicieza and Scott Lobdell, which would pass through each issue, promising an event of lasting consequence to the X-Men's universe. And if the X-fans weren't already chomping at the bit, the powers that be enlisted an all-star array of artists, including the likes of John Romita Jr., Andy and Adam Kubert, Jae Lee, Chris Sprouse, Brandon Peterson, and Paul Smith. The result was a flashy, dramatic battle that altered the life of not just one major mutant player, but three, as Wolverine and Magneto were injured beyond measure, and Professor Xavier crossed over a moral line he had vowed never to tread.

144-145

The Story

In the aftermath of a ferocious battle with Magneto, Wolverine attempts to recover after having the adamantium ripped from his skeleton...

The X-Men had pushed Magneto too far. He had tried to warn them and even visited the funeral of their loved one, Illyana Rasputin, and successfully recruited Illyana's brother, the mutant known as Colossus to his cause, but Charles Xavier and the rest of his X-Men had yet again opposed him. After returning to his space satellite—the mutant haven he had dubbed "Avalon"—Magneto realized it wasn't just the X-Men who were scheming against him. The humans were up to their old tricks as well.

The United Nations Security Council had voted, and their decision was clear: It was time to take defensive measures against Magneto and his cohorts. One by one, satellites hovering all around Earth's orbit lit up, creating a mesh of protective electromagnetic fire, which prevented Magneto from ever venturing to his home planet. But all it did was make him angry.

Generating a massive magnetic pulse strong enough to short out all the satellites, Magneto also succeeded in temporarily shutting down Earth's entire electronic power grid. As buildings all over the globe lost electricity, the X-Men could no longer idly stand by. It was time for them to attack and they would do so in full force. Professor X led their army, their paralyzed founder donning a special alien exoskeleton that allowed him to walk for the first time in years.

Storming Magneto's Avalon home, the heroes fought their way through his army of acolytes, until they were finally faced with the master of magnetism himself.

As the battle raged on, Wolverine attacked his old foe, only to have an angered Magneto use his powers to pull the adamantium that was bonded to Logan's bones out of the feral mutant's body through his pores. With Logan reeling in excruciating pain, Professor X lashed out at Magnus in the only way he knew how, virtually lobotomizing his longtime rival with a devastating psychic strike. With Magneto defeated, the X-Men quickly loaded Logan back into their spacecraft, and rocketed home towards Earth, praying that their friend would survive the journey.

As they entered Earth's atmosphere and Wolverine's broken body attempted to mend itself, Phoenix linked her mind with his, as well as that of Professor Xavier, in an attempt to ease Wolverine's psychic trauma (1). Entering the landscape of Logan's tortured mind, Jean and Xavier bore witness to a nightmare concoction of fragments of Wolverine's many past battles against the likes of Sabretooth and Lady Deathstrike. They witnessed Logan's time in the clutches of the corrupt Weapon X program (2), as well as his torture at the hands of the Reavers.

"Logan, your life-graphs had bottomed out on the Medi-unit scanners..."

"...y-you came back—for me?"

Meanwhile, back in the physical plane, the X-Men's craft entered a horrific storm, and subsequently lost cabin pressure. As a hatch blew open out of a side of the shuttle, Logan awoke suddenly, grabbing Jean Grey's wrist just in time to save her from being sucked out of the aircraft (3). And just as suddenly as it had arrived, the storm fizzled out, and soon the X-Men arrived back at Westchester, safe and sound.

As the rest of his teammates returned to life as usual, Logan found getting back into the swing of things a bit difficult at first. Ignoring his doctor's orders and resuming his Danger Room workouts, Wolverine was surprised to find that he was moving slower and with less confidence than before (4). But what really shocked him was when he instinctively tried to pop his claws, and jagged bones shot out from his forearms instead. Later, after talking his new condition over with his old sidekick Jubilee (5), Logan realized that he had become a liability to his team. And so that night, in his usual style, Wolverine packed up his things and set out on the open road, unsure of his destination (6).

ONSLAUGHT

It had been biding its time for months. After Professor X had altered Magneto's mind during the Fatal Attractions adventure, the evil in Magneto's core had been separated from his personality. However, energy doesn't just disappear. Magneto's evil psyche found a home deep in Professor X's subconscious, and awaited its chance to strike.

Finally the merge was complete. Magneto's evil side and the dark corners of Professor X's own mind formed into one: A malevolent entity calling himself Onslaught, his appearance a ferocious take on Magneto's own costume. Onslaught began to plot, with global domination in mind. The entity started to appear to friends and relatives of Professor X, terrifying the normally unstoppable Juggernaut and appealing to Jean Grey, hoping to persuade her to side with his cause. After Jean denied him the first time, Onslaught sought again to recruit her, this time alongside the rest of the X-Men, including Iceman, Cannonball, Beast, Gambit, Storm, Bishop, Cyclops, and Wolverine. His pleas fell on deaf ears, for the X-Men were used to hearing this sort of power-mad rhetoric from the many megalomaniac opponents they'd faced over the years. However, Onslaught was certainly not a typical foe.

Swatting his former students as if they were flies, Onslaught departed the X-Men's mansion to further his master plan. Onslaught's mutant abilities proved too powerful for the Fantastic Four, the Avengers, and Spider-Man. But in a final, desperate play to rid the world of Onslaught's evil, the heroes of the Marvel Universe gathered together, united against their common foe.

Onslaught had evolved into a state of pure psionic energy, becoming a seemingly unstoppable force of nature. However, through a period of violent trial and error, the heroes realized that if they flung themselves into the void of Onslaught's very being, the resulting backlash would hurt the villain. Perhaps, if enough heroes participated, the shock would prove too much for Onslaught, and he would be destroyed.

FIRST APPEARANCE
X-Man #15

REAL NAME *Not applicable*

OCCUPATION *Would-be world conqueror*

BASE *New York City*

AFFILIATIONS *Employer of Gateway, Post, Blob, Mimic, Holocaust, and Dark Beast. Controller of Sentinel army.*

POWERS/WEAPONS *Xavier's mental abilities combined with Magneto's powers of magnetism. Ability to induce illusions or amnesia. Telekinetic powers.*

As Wolverine and the X-Men assaulted Onslaught with one last barrage of mutant energy, the Fantastic Four, Avengers, and Incredible Hulk flung themselves at the beast, making what they assumed would be the ultimate sacrifice, and destroying this mutant cancer for good.

FIRST APPEARANCE
New Mutants #98

REAL NAME Tyler Dayspring

OCCUPATION Would-be world conqueror, freedom fighter, arms dealer

BASE Egypt

AFFILIATIONS Leader of the Dark Riders, formerly New Canaanites, Clan Chosen

POWERS/WEAPONS Mutant ability to project other's thoughts as holograms.

Born in a future where the malignant overseer Apocalypse ruled all but a rebellious few, it was no surprise that Tyler Dayspring would eventually fall under the evil mutant's influence. When he was brainwashed by Stryfe, a clone of his father Cable, Tyler's world view was perverted, and he became a loyal follower of Apocalypse. Using a time nexus hidden within Niagara Falls, Tyler traveled back to the present, and adopted the name Genesis, intent on seeing his lord and master rise in this "primitive" reality. This would prove a tough task indeed, as at that time, Apocalypse had seemingly died. But as everyone knows, an Apocalypse needs Horsemen. Amassing his own Dark Riders, Genesis came upon the idea of recruiting Wolverine to his cause, finding the feral mutant to be a perfect fit for role of the Horseman called Death. But there was a minor flaw in Genesis's mind's eye—Wolverine now lacked his formidable adamantium enhancements.

①

He hailed from a dystopian future. He was the adopted son of the mutant Cable, and a sworn minion of the evil Apocalypse. He was...

GENESIS

RRRRRRR...

① Capturing Logan, and attempting to re-bond his skeleton to adamantium that he had stolen from the villain Cyber, Genesis was angered to discover that Wolverine was somehow willing the process to fail. Logan was finally able to overload the machines and cause a massive explosion.

② Meanwhile, in his Egyptian hideout, Genesis had concocted a huge device that literally sucked the life energies out of hundreds of innocents, transferring them into the body of the lifeless Apocalypse.

③ Surviving the explosion, Logan emerged from the flames. However the bonding process had taken its toll on him, giving him the appearance of a wild animal.

④ Using his feral instincts and his natural bone claws, Logan made short work of the Dark Riders as his fellow X-Man Cannonball jumped into action, attempting to sabotage Apocalypse's resurrection. Wolverine then killed Genesis in a fit of pure animal rage.

ELEKTRA

Even in the darkest parts of the world, Elektra's name is only whispered. Because even the lowest of the low aren't brave, or desperate, enough to utter it at full volume. To her victims she is death incarnate, the perfect assassin. To the blind Super Hero Daredevil, she is a true love, and a missed opportunity. And to Wolverine, she is something rare indeed— she is a friend.

TRUSTED ALLIES

Already familiar with each other from a lifetime of running with similar crowds, Wolverine and Elektra didn't become close friends until after Elektra's death at the hands of the villain Bullseye. Resurreced and starting her life anew alongside the spirit of her deceased sensei Stick, Elektra reached out to Wolverine when he was reduced to not much more than a mere animal. Left in a primal state by the twisted mutant Genesis, Logan was indeed in need of a friend, and this new altruistic Elektra filled that void perfectly.

A WARRIOR'S TALE

As a young girl, Elektra's rich father arranged for training in martial arts and gymnastics by a variety of instructors. After her father's violent death, Elektra opted to continue those studies with a renewed fervor, attempting to join the ranks of the elite noble warriors known as the Chaste. However, her inner rage betrayed her, and soon she was shamefully cast out of their midst. Seeking solace among the corrupt ninja known as the Hand, Elektra became one of their premier assassins, before later seeing the error of her ways.

Despite their origins as a defensive weapon, sais become the ultimate killing tool in Elektra's capable hands.

FIRST APPEARANCE
Daredevil #168

REAL NAME *Elektra Natchios*

OCCUPATION Assassin

BASE *Mobile*

AFFILIATIONS *formerly the Hand, the Chaste*

POWERS/WEAPONS *Expert martial artist. Olympic-level athlete and gymnast. Master of sai and other martial arts weapons*

OLD WOUNDS

As Elektra and her disembodied master Stick helped Logan through his transformation at the hands of Genesis, Elektra began to realize how much she had in common with the feral mutant. Soon the two began to reveal a bit more about themselves to each other. Wolverine took Elektra on his annual pilgrimage to the cabin that he had shared with Silver Fox in the Canadian Rockies, and Elektra brought Logan home to Greece, to meet what remained of her shattered family.

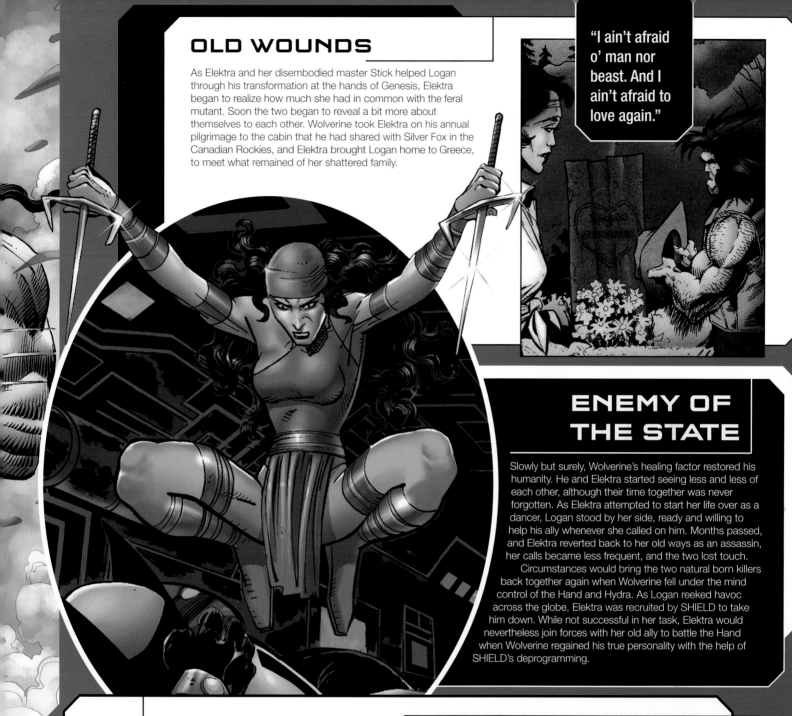

"I ain't afraid o' man nor beast. And I ain't afraid to love again."

ENEMY OF THE STATE

Slowly but surely, Wolverine's healing factor restored his humanity. He and Elektra started seeing less and less of each other, although their time together was never forgotten. As Elektra attempted to start her life over as a dancer, Logan stood by her side, ready and willing to help his ally whenever she called on him. Months passed, and Elektra reverted back to her old ways as an assassin, her calls became less frequent, and the two lost touch.
　　Circumstances would bring the two natural born killers back together again when Wolverine fell under the mind control of the Hand and Hydra. As Logan reeked havoc across the globe, Elektra was recruited by SHIELD to take him down. While not successful in her task, Elektra would nevertheless join forces with her old ally to battle the Hand when Wolverine regained his true personality with the help of SHIELD's deprogramming.

IMPOSTER

While meditating at her home in Osaka, Japan, Elektra was shocked when she was attacked by a woman who looked identical to her. Despite her doppelganger's use of super powers, Elektra proved the more efficient fighter, and stabbing her foe in the chest, she killed her. As her attacker's limp body slowly morphed into its true form, it became clear to Elektra what she was up against. Her failed assassin was a Skrull, a member of an alien race of shape-shifters and would-be conquerors. After being attacked by several more Skrulls, Elektra finally fell in battle, and was replaced by a duplicate who slowly maneuvered her back into league with the Hand, where she eventually came into conflict with Wolverine and the New Avengers.

Death

To fulfill his twisted vision of the survival of the fittest, the evil mutant Apocalypse has recruited many Horsemen, but none more formidable than Wolverine as Death.

Wolverine never took kindly to being kidnapped. When he and his fellow X-Men were frozen in suspended animation in outer space while returning home from a battle with the planet-devouring giant Galactus, Wolverine wasn't too happy to discover that he had been abducted. He was brought before En Sabah Nur, alias Apocalypse, the ancient evil mutant hiding behind a human visage. Wolverine despised Apocalypse for all his previous battles with the X-Men and initially rejected the mutant's offer to join him as one of his reprogrammed henchmen known as the Horsemen. However, that was before Sabretooth came on the scene.

In accordance with his obsession with the survival of the fittest, Apocalypse had abducted both Wolverine and Sabretooth. He forced the two rival mutants into combat, not caring that Wolverine was at a disadvantage. Sabretooth's bones were laced with adamantium, but Wolverine had had the super-hard metal stripped from his bones years ago.

As Death, Wolverine was brainwashed and his powers were augmented. With his adamantium reinstated, his new moniker suddenly became more than appropriate.

After defeating Sabretooth in Apocalypse's arena, Wolverine accepted his fate as a Horseman in order to prevent a bloodthirsty monster like Sabretooth from taking the role. Wolverine underwent a painful operation that transferred Sabretooth's adamantium into his own body, lacing his bones and claws with the metal once more. He emerged with his mind conditioned to only one reality: total loyalty to his master Apocalypse.

As Apocalypse's new lapdog Death, Wolverine sought to help his master speed up the evolutionary process. His first order was to destroy a race of children called the Mannites, a mission that brought him into conflict with the X-Men. Knowing the group's weaknesses, Death cut a bloody swath through the team, even as the heroes returned to battle him time and again. However, he began to weaken as he was hunted through the old abandoned Morlock tunnels under the Xavier Institute by his former teammates Jubilee, Kitty Pryde, and Angel. This allowed the telepathic mutant Psylocke to get a grip on Wolverine's mind, pushing his true personality to the forefront. Battling with his feral nature, Wolverine returned to his old self, now once again possessing his adamantium claws.

Another of Death's initial errands for Apocalypse was to track down the super-strong behemoth known as the Hulk. Despite Death's new enhancements, he managed to let his prey escape him.

Due to his tendency to stay in the shadows and remain shrouded in a hood and scarf, Wolverine kept his identity secret while masquerading as Death. However, during a battle with Colossus, Death was struck in the face, revealing his alter ego to his former friends. Knowing as much about their opponent as he knew about them, the X-Men were soon able to turn the tables on Death.

IT'S BIRTH WAS A FLUKE, A SECRET SEED PLANTED ONLY TO BEAR THE FRUITS OF CORRUPTION. BUT THE ROOTS OF WEAPON X REACHED MUCH DEEPER THAN EVEN WOLVERINE REALIZED.

Wolverine assumed he was the first, that Experiment X had been so-called because of Logan's inherent X-Factor, the gene that made him a mutant. But with a past full of dark surprises and deadly secrets, Wolverine should have learned not to make assumptions.

In reality, the X was a simple Roman numeral and Wolverine was the tenth in a long line of experiments, dating back to 1945. While exploring the remnants of a liberated concentration camp, a man named Professor Thorton had come across the hidden lab of evil mutant geneticist Mr. Sinister. Combining Thorton's discovery with information taken from the government's Operation: Rebirth (later dubbed Weapon I), the Weapon Plus program was born, a secret government institution shared between Canada and the United States.

By the time the project neared it's tenth incarnation, the mysterious Professor Thorton was taking orders from his even more enigmatic superior, a lupine mutant named Romulus. His motives questionable at best, Romulus helped pervert the clandestine Weapon X institution to suit his own devious ways, taking particular interest in their test subject Logan.

In recent years, the Weapon Plus program has fallen into the hands of the mutant hating John Sublime, and it has continued its operations, experimenting with more and more powerful weapons.

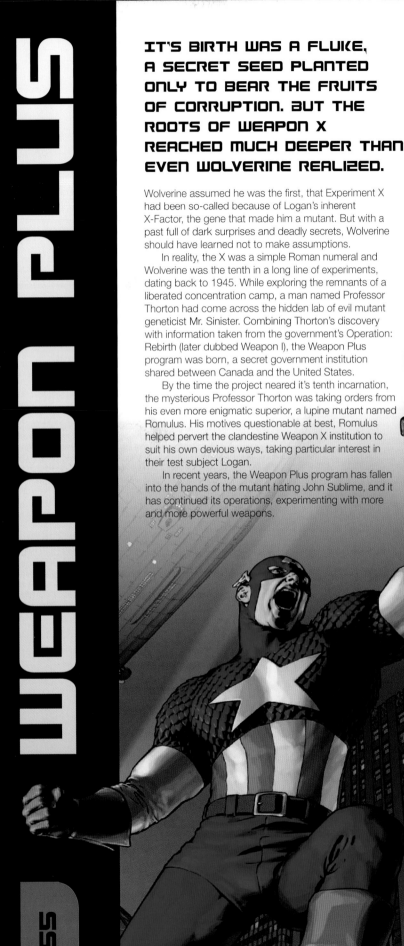

WEAPON I

Steve Rogers had no idea what the government was up to. He just did his duty and volunteered to be injected with a super-serum that transformed him into the hero Captain America. No one bothered to inform him of the dozens of African American military men who had been experimented on against their will to create that serum, or of the first successful Captain America, Isaiah Bradley. And no one informed him that the details of his experiment would later be exploited by the Weapon Plus program.

WEAPON II-IV

In an attempt to recreate the Captain America serum from partial notes and added information from the labs of Mr. Sinister, Professor Thorton and his crew originally began their experiments on animals, creating Weapons II, III and IV.

WEAPON V-VI

Thorton and the Weapon Plus team were no longer satisfied with experimenting on animals. For the next two Weapons in their program, live human subjects were utilized, Thorton opting only to experiment on various ethnic minorities.

WEAPON VII

Working in tandem with Romulus, the Weapon Plus team decided to add brainwashing and emotional manipulation to their already disturbing program. Romulus helped mold the child Frank Simpson into a mentally unstable killing machine, and he grew up into a perfect match for the government's new super-soldier program, Project: Homegrown, which changed Simpson into the demented powerhouse Nuke.

WEAPON VIII-IX

With the success of the mentally unbalanced Nuke paving the way for more similar test subjects, Weapons VIII and IX utilized criminals and psychopaths as cannon fodder for their various experiments and augmentations.

THE WORLD

It's a square mile of experimental micro-reality. With its own culture, history, and religion, and the uncanny ability to freeze time within its walls, the World is a feat of human accomplishment. If only its primary goal wasn't to destroy all of mutantkind.

The brainchild of Weapon Plus director John Sublime, the World was mostly put out of commission by the team of Wolverine, Fantomex, and Cyclops, when they broke into its inner chambers to hunt the dangerous Weapon XV.

WEAPON X

Although Logan wasn't the only test subject of Weapon X, he was their greatest success—and their greatest failure. After he escaped from his imprisonment at the hands of Romulus, Professor Thorton. and Canada's Department K, Logan discovered that another lupine mutant named the Native had also been a guinea pig for that phase of the Weapon Plus. In addition, Wade Wilson, the mercenary for hire known as Deadpool, was also a product of Weapon X's tampering, and had been given a healing factor from Logan's own DNA.

X-23

The Weapon X program declined after Logan's escape, but it was reborn on more than one occasion. Eventually, a splintered faction of the organization set out to create the ultimate mercenary for hire, and cloned Logan's DNA. The result was X-23 a young female version of Wolverine who followed in her predecessor's footsteps and escaped her captivity, carving up anyone foolish enough to try and stop her.

WEAPON XI-XII

Wolverine and the X-Men have yet to discover any information about the mutant codenamed Weapon XI, but unfortunately, they're very aware of Weapon XII. Also known as the Huntsman, Weapon XII was let loose during a train wreck inside the Eurotunnel. There he was defeated by Fantomex and a few of the X-Men, but not before the powerful mutant murdered X-alumni Darkstar.

WEAPON XIII

An international criminal who has been around for years, just under the radar of the system, he would tell you his name is Fantomex. But you shouldn't believe a thing he says. A brilliant mind developed in the labs of Weapon Plus, Fantomex was supposed to be a Super Hero. With the intent of making him the "bad boy" of his public Super Sentinel squad, John Sublime helped shape the persona of Fantomex, only to have his creation rebel, and start his own life as an independent mercenary.

WEAPON XIV

They were planted inside the X-Men's home, and no one had a clue. Five identical teenage clones of Emma Frost called the Stepford Cuckoos, each with powerful psi-talents, attended classes with the rest of the mutant youth at the Xavier Institute. Two of them died during various school scandals, but the Cuckoos never dreamed they were merely a handful of the thousand mutant clones created as part of John Sublime's Weapon XIV project.

WEAPON XV

Hatched in the mammoth Petri dish that was the World, Weapon XV was the perfect killing machine with his sights set on the entire mutant population. Able to adapt his programming to defeat any foe, Weapon XV was meant to be a Super Sentinel until Wolverine destroyed him in an explosion when the two faced off in a government satellite.

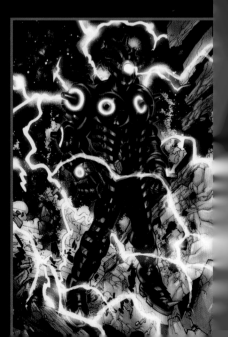

A PAWN IN THE GORGON'S DEADLY GAME, WOLVERINE BECAME THE ENEMY OF THE STATE.

THE STORY

A group of men used Mariko's kidnapped cousin to lure Logan all the way back to Japan. Unfortunately Wolverine's enhanced senses didn't smell a setup until it was too late. Ambushed by a horde of Hand ninjas, Logan put up a valiant fight until, seemingly out of nowhere, the superhuman Gorgon joined the battle. Before Wolverine knew what was going on, Gorgon ran him through with a sword, killing the mutant before his body had a chance to heal the new wound.

Gorgon's plan was to convert Wolverine into his own killing machine. Using an ancient Hand resurrection ritual, Gorgon and his Hand and Hydra compatriots took over Wolverine's mind. Awaking aboard a SHIELD helicarrier with violent thoughts that were not his own running through his brain, Logan wreaked havoc on the ship and then escaped. He had become Hydra's star errand boy. Wolverine was now public enemy number one, so SHIELD brought in a big gun to deal with him—his old friend, Elektra. Meanwhile, Hydra decided to try their brainwashing techniques on some new subjects...

DEPROGRAMMING

Wolverine was a hard nut to crack. Although he committed the occasional good deed while under the Hand's spell, the resurrection ritual had created a deep-seated sense of loyalty to the Hand and Hydra. After taking Logan captive, SHIELD experimented on the mutant by forcing him to live virtual reality scenarios over and over. Finally, during an attack on the SHIELD helicarrier by some of Logan's former allies—who had been brainwashed like him—Wolverine rejected the Hand's programming and donned his costume once again, determined to bring down those who had manipulated his friends.

Wolverine eventually overcame his brainwashing, and was forced to fight the super-fast mutant Northstar and Elektra, who had both been brainwashed to the Hand's cause.

THE GORGON

Tomi Shishido was a super-intelligent mutant with the power to turn his victims into stone with a glance. He joined the Hand and proved his dedication by killing himself in order to become their reborn pawn. Now known as the Gorgon, Tomi quickly ascended the Hand's ranks, seizing the opportunity to join with the terrorist cell Hydra.

While the Gorgon relaxed in his Manhattan apartment, Wolverine battled his way back to his true persona, taking out the brainwashed Northstar in the process. Out for revenge against his killers, Logan piloted a giant Sentinel robot directly into the Hand's home base. There he killed hundreds of Hand operatives, and freed Elektra, who had also overcome her brainwashing. Partners once again, Logan and Elektra took their fight directly to Gorgon's home, but he turned the tables on them. Using Elektra to determine the location of SHIELD commander Nick Fury, Gorgon teleported to Fury's secret New York infirmary. Gorgon would have decapitated Fury, but for Logan's timely intervention via jetpack. Gorgon and Wolverine fought over the Manhattan skyline until Logan tricked his opponent into seeing his own reflection in Wolverine's adamantium claws. As Gorgon turned to stone, Wolverine shattered his remains, getting revenge for Mariko's family.

TIMELINE

"We'll find out who did this. And then we'll avenge it."

MISSION NUMBER 1

The Avengers had been disassembled. After former member Scarlet Witch had gone insane and killed several of them, the legendary team had become a thing of the past. They would have stayed that way if the Raft hadn't exploded.

As Luke Cage and Spider-Woman Jessica Drew toured this maximum holding facility, the criminal Electro attacked and freed all of the dangerous super-powered inmates. Iron Man, Spider-Man, and Captain America rushed to the prison to lend a hand, then embarked on a mission to the Savage Land, to track down Electro's employers. There they joined with Wolverine, already hot on the same trail, and the New Avengers were formed. The team took down the powerful mutant Sauron, and a corrupt branch of the government agency SHIELD.

REGISTRATION

When the Super Hero Registration Act was passed, a Civil War broke out between the nation's masked crime fighters. As torn as any other faction of heroes, the Avengers split into two divisions: the Mighty Avengers organized by Iron Man, a staunch supporter of registering heroes with the government, and Captain America's Secret Avengers, a team of heroes operating from the shadows, and protesting the government's involvement in their lives. Although he was busy tracking down the villain Nitro during the majority of the Civil War, when the dust had settled, Wolverine resumed his role alongside the Secret Avengers, believing in the group's noble cause. Continually on the run from the law, this new batch of Secret Avengers was later augmented by new members Echo, Iron Fist, Dr. Strange, and the second hero to call himself Ronin.

THE OLD AVENGERS

It began with a ragtag mismatched group of heroes: the armored Iron Man, the shrinking Ant-Man and Wasp, god of thunder Thor, and even the rampaging Incredible Hulk. United together by circumstance, and kept together by necessity, the team wouldn't quite blossom until they unearthed World War II hero Captain America, who was frozen in a block of ice at the ocean's floor, trapped in suspended animation at his prime. Once revived, Cap quickly became the uncontested leader, and served as a constant inspiration to the rest of the team. As members came and went, the team took up residence off Manhattan's Central Park in an impressive mansion supplied by Iron Man's alter ego, billionaire Tony Stark. It was there that the team quickly became the lauded guardians of all mankind and Earth's mightiest heroes—the Avengers.

ECHO

The deaf Maya Lopez possesses photographic reflexes that allow her to mimic physical movements she sees others perform. She utilized this talent as a crime fighter called Echo after being manipulated by the criminal Kingpin into hunting the hero Daredevil.

RONIN

Originally Echo in disguise, the identity of the wandering samurai Ronin was passed on to former Avenger Hawkeye when he returned from the seeming grave. Though master of the bow and arrow, as Ronin, Clint Barton now relies mostly on his martial art skills.

IRON FIST

Danny Rand is the newest in a long line of martial artists possessing the ability to channel their chi into a rock hard fist of fury. He uses his powers as well as his bank account to aid the Secret Avengers, even funding a new hideout for the clandestine team.

DR. STRANGE

The former Sorcerer Supreme of the Marvel Universe, Dr. Stephen Strange recently abandoned his title after using a darker variety of his magic powers in battle. However, before leaving the New Avengers, Strange had been offering his mystically shrouded home to them as a refuge.

SPIDER-MAN

When Peter Parker was bitten by a radioactive spider, granting him the proportionate powers of the arachnid, his life was turned upside down as he became the wall-crawling hero Spider-Man. Originally a supporter of Iron Man's registration act, Spidey realized the error of his ways and went on the run with the Avengers.

LUKE CAGE

Assuming a leadership role in the New Avengers after the death of Captain America, Luke Cage uses his intelligence, tough attitude and near-invulnerable skin to become an influential voice in his team's secret operations. A reformed criminal who was granted his powers in an experimental operation, Cage has been on both sides of the law before, and therefore is unwavering in his opposition to the Super Hero Registration Act.

WOLVERINE

Despite being a mutant and exempt from the Registration Act, Wolverine has stuck by his fellow New Avengers until the present day. Always exhibiting a fierce sense of loyalty, Logan wholeheartedly supports the Secret Avengers' cause, and will do everything in his power to fight against this new form of government oppression.

The Scarlet Witch had gone insane. A former Avenger and the daughter of Magneto, Wanda Maximoff had been spiraling away from sanity for years, and hit rock bottom when she single-handedly disassembled the Avengers, killing several of their members and destroying their home. As the other heroes decided what to do about their old friend, Wanda stretched her reality warping abilities to their fullest, and recreated the universe in her own image.

THE HOUSE OF M

No longer the hated minority, mutants were now the abundant majority in a brave new world led by Magneto's royal family.

Awaking in this new World of M with all his old memories intact, Wolverine discovered that he was now an agent of SHIELD.

Wolverine had been mind-wiped before, and he had no intention of repeating that fate. Abandoning his position in the Magneto-run government organization SHIELD, Wolverine traveled to Manhattan, deciding to seek out past allies. As he hunted for Charles Xavier, Wolverine was being hunted himself by his old government colleagues. He narrowly escaped the agents with the help of the sudden appearance of the teleporter Cloak. Logan stumbled upon the Human Resistance Movement, led by strong man Luke Cage. As Magneto's human-hunting Sentinels pursued the underground team, Wolverine and company successfully recruited Spider-Man, Daredevil, the X-Men, and a host of others, and then stormed Magneto's Genoshan island home.

Hitching a ride inside a commandeered Sentinel, the heroes struggled valiantly against Magneto's forces, finally showing the villain the truth of the situation. With his past memories restored, Magneto realized that his daughter had been coerced into creating this new reality by her brother, the former Avenger Quicksilver. Magneto attacked his son and to avoid further conflict, the Scarlet Witch restored the world to its true form, with one major difference: she removed the powers of nearly every living mutant on Earth.

With all of his past memories restored for the first time in his entire life, Logan escaped SHIELD by literally throwing himself off their helicarrier.

The World of M was overseen by Magneto and his royal family, consisting of his daughters, Scarlet Witch and Polaris, and his son, Quicksilver. His rule was looked upon favorably by the vast majority of the mutants under his thrall, however this was not a sentiment shared by their *Homo sapiens* relatives. Humans were oppressed in this new reality in much the same way that mutants had been in the previous one.

When staging their attack on the House of M, the Human Resistance had hidden inside a Sentinel. Magneto easily halted it with his magnetic powers.

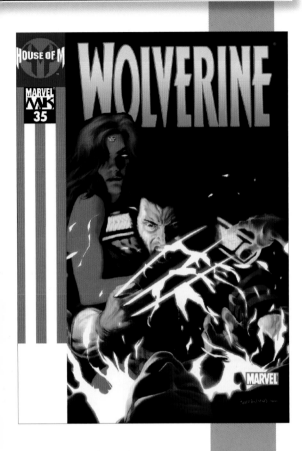

WOLVERINE #35

"Ever since the end of the war, I've just been killin' time... but now, I'm gonna' kill you. An' this time... yer gonna stay dead."

(WOLVERINE)

MAIN CHARACTERS: Wolverine, Mystique, Sebastian Shaw
SUPPORTING CHARACTERS: SHIELD agents, human soldiers, Jessica Drew
LOCATIONS: SHIELD helicarrier; Unified Steel Corp.

Publication date
December, 2005

Editor-in-chief
Joe Quesada

Cover artist
Kaare Andrews

Writer
Daniel Way

Penciller
Javier Saltares

Inker
Mark Texeira

Colorist
Paul Mounts

Letterer
Randy Gentile

Background

Marvel was bringing back the event. After Joe Quesada was promoted to Editor-in-chief at Marvel, he quickly began to create a mix of style and substance, insisting his writers stop dwelling on the minutiae of continuity, and reinstating storytelling as the backbone of all the company's line of books. As character development and innovative plots became the norm, and the Marvel Universe once again had a strong base to build upon, Quesada decided to bring back the epic crossovers that fans had been used to seeing throughout the 1990s.

After Nick Fury dabbled in his Secret War and the Avengers disassembled, the scene was set for an even more massive crossover as audiences began to warm up to these types of large-scale stories. So superstar writer Brian Michael Bendis, alongside popular artist Olivier Coipel were commissioned to create *The House of M*, an eight-part miniseries that would place the Marvel heroes in an alternate universe fashioned by the unhinged Scarlet Witch. A great success for all involved, *The House of M* featured tie-ins throughout the Marvel universe, including a three-issue story arc in the pages of Wolverine's own title.

The Story

In the altered World of M, Sebastian Shaw and Mystique try to piece together just why Logan quit his job as SHIELD super-spy...

1

2

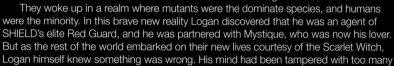

3

9

Longtime Avenger Wanda Maximoff, also known as the Scarlet Witch, hadn't liked the game, so she decided to make up her own rules. Mentally unhinged for years, the daughter of Magneto had finally snapped, killing several members of her Super Hero team in the process. As the heroes of the world united to decide their former friend's fate, the Scarlet Witch—with a bit of coaching from her brother Quicksilver—used her magical abilities to recreate the entire Marvel Universe in her own image.

They woke up in a realm where mutants were the dominate species, and humans were the minority. In this brave new reality Logan discovered that he was an agent of SHIELD's elite Red Guard, and he was partnered with Mystique, who was now his lover. But as the rest of the world embarked on their new lives courtesy of the Scarlet Witch, Logan himself knew something was wrong. His mind had been tampered with too many times in the past, and suddenly he remembered everything. Not only did he recall how the world used to be before Wanda's interference, but he also remembered his entire history, all the twists and turns his healing factor and many memory implants had forced him to forget. So he decided to set things straight. And he jumped right off the side of the SHIELD helicarrier and plummeted to the Earth below.

To the rest of the world, unaware that they'd ever existed in a different reality, Logan's sudden bail out came as quite a mystery. His direct superior, Sebastian Shaw, wasn't about to let an event like this go by without some sort of explanation, so he called Mystique into his office and began to interrogate her about the situation. However, Mystique was just as in the dark as he was. She had gone to Logan's room, only to find her lover gone **(1)**. All she could report were the events of recent weeks, and the details of a party in Mexico: Mystique and Logan had been assigned as security for a mutant gala that was celebrating the new human-hunting Sentinel that the Mexican government had recently acquired. Logan was drinking as usual—the natural-born warrior depressed that there were no longer any enemies to fight—when suddenly the party was attacked, and the Sentinel was stolen. Mystique saw the enemy's face before he departed. He was a man from Logan's past, one thought long dead. Logan's former drill sergeant, Nick Fury.

As Shaw became more and more irate with Mystique's story **(2)**, he had her thrown into the brig for not reporting Logan's departure when she first had the chance. Meanwhile, Shaw met with one of his scientists, to see if it was possible for Fury to still be alive **(3)**. Getting no concrete answers, he paid a visit to Mystique's cell, to hear more of her side of the story. As Mystique once again began to spin her yarn, she talked about how Logan trailed the stolen Sentinel to a base where it had been disassembled **(4)**. After fighting off the armed guards he encountered there **(5)**, Logan stormed into the office of Nick Fury himself **(6)**. Realizing that the man he was talking to was merely a hologram **(7)**, Logan narrowly escaped the building as Fury seemingly triggered its detonation from afar **(8)**, encouraging Logan to hunt down and kill his old enemy.

And that was all Shaw needed to hear. He had figured it all out **(9)**. Nick Fury wasn't back from the dead at all. Mystique had been using her shape-changing powers to impersonate him **(10)**, engaging Logan in a complex web of intrigue versus an imaginary opponent, all in an attempt to lift him out of his life's depression. Still unsure of why Logan jumped ship, Shaw set Mystique free, ordering her to bring in the man she may well have driven away **(11)**.

"You sent him on this chase...

...You bring him back."

4

5

6

7

8

11

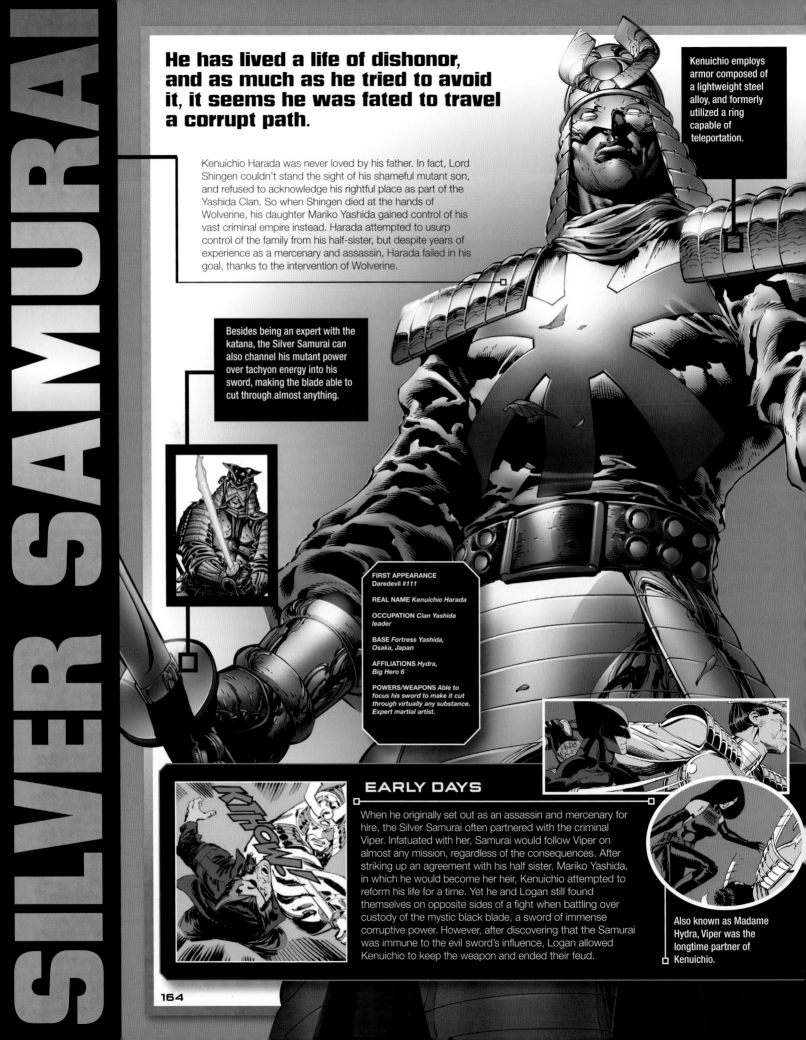

SILVER SAMURAI

He has lived a life of dishonor, and as much as he tried to avoid it, it seems he was fated to travel a corrupt path.

Kenuichio Harada was never loved by his father. In fact, Lord Shingen couldn't stand the sight of his shameful mutant son, and refused to acknowledge his rightful place as part of the Yashida Clan. So when Shingen died at the hands of Wolverine, his daughter Mariko Yashida gained control of his vast criminal empire instead. Harada attempted to usurp control of the family from his half-sister, but despite years of experience as a mercenary and assassin, Harada failed in his goal, thanks to the intervention of Wolverine.

Besides being an expert with the katana, the Silver Samurai can also channel his mutant power over tachyon energy into his sword, making the blade able to cut through almost anything.

Kenuichio employs armor composed of a lightweight steel alloy, and formerly utilized a ring capable of teleportation.

FIRST APPEARANCE
Daredevil #111

REAL NAME *Kenuichio Harada*

OCCUPATION *Clan Yashida leader*

BASE *Fortress Yashida, Osaka, Japan*

AFFILIATIONS *Hydra, Big Hero 6*

POWERS/WEAPONS *Able to focus his sword to make it cut through virtually any substance. Expert martial artist.*

EARLY DAYS

When he originally set out as an assassin and mercenary for hire, the Silver Samurai often partnered with the criminal Viper. Infatuated with her, Samurai would follow Viper on almost any mission, regardless of the consequences. After striking up an agreement with his half sister, Mariko Yashida, in which he would become her heir, Kenuichio attempted to reform his life for a time. Yet he and Logan still found themselves on opposite sides of a fight when battling over custody of the mystic black blade, a sword of immense corruptive power. However, after discovering that the Samurai was immune to the evil sword's influence, Logan allowed Kenuichio to keep the weapon and ended their feud.

Also known as Madame Hydra, Viper was the longtime partner of Kenuichio.

LOSING A HAND

When his memories were restored to him during the House of M event, Wolverine set out with a long list of people he needed to settle scores with. One of those people was Kenuichio Harada. Armed and ready in his Silver Samurai uniform, Kenuichio was busy escorting the Prime Minister of Japan as the captain for his personal security cadre. As SHIELD kept tabs on Wolverine, not knowing who the mutant's first target would be, Logan decided to attack Harada in a tunnel underneath Tokyo.

As the two began to fight, the Prime Minister and his entourage fled the tunnel to safety, to the relief of the observing SHIELD personnel. Soon, Kenuichio used his vaunted skills to run Wolverine through, which gave Logan just the opportunity he needed. Grabbing Kenuichio's arm, Wolverine raised his other claw, and chopped off the Silver Samurai's hand at the wrist. As the Silver Samurai gave Wolverine the answers he needed, Logan pulled the sword out from his own stomach, and trudged away.

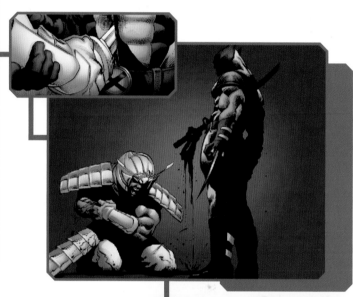

"MUCH AS I REGRET DOIN' IT, THERE'S ONLY ONE WAY TO DISARM A SAMURAI"

"PERMANENTLY"

BLOOD DEBT

After Mariko's death, Kenuichio assumed leadership of the Yashida Clan, slowly corroding the formerly powerful Japanese institution into a laughable amateur production. Reduced to an almost feeble drunk, the Silver Samurai appealed to Logan for help when two rival criminal brothers, Haan and Gom Kaishek began to vie for his criminal territory. Logan soon found himself in the middle of a gang war, with the lives of his ward Amiko, and his former lover Yukio hanging in the balance. Ultimately, Logan discovered that Haan and Gom's sister Kia was the real threat to be dealt with.

WOLVERINE'S
CIVIL WAR

It was an epic conflict that pitted brother against brother. A battle between heroes the likes of which the Marvel Universe had never witnessed. It was the Super Hero Civil War, and Wolverine was caught right in the middle.

It was a choice the heroes never thought they'd have to make. When a conflict between the young heroes known as the New Warriors and a group of Super Villains escalated into the destruction of a school and the surrounding small town of Stamford, Connecticut, civilians became infuriated, and needed a place to direct their anger. Soon Congress provided the answer and passed the Super Hero Registration Act, creating a law that required all superhumans to register their powers with the United States government or face incarceration. Those willing to expose their secret identities to the authorities would be placed in the Initiative program, and be trained to serve their country as part of a government sponsored Super Hero team. Needless to say, this controversial new law divided the Super Hero community in half, the pro-registration side filing in behind Iron Man, while the dissenters rallied behind the voice of freedom, Captain America.

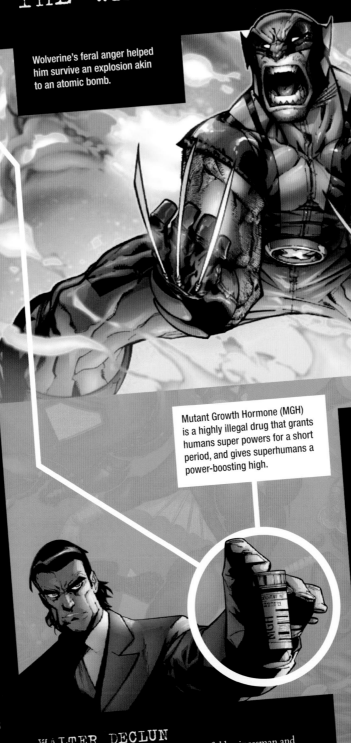

"LOOKS LIKE THE SHORTEST OF THE X-MEN'S GONE THE WAY OF ALL FLESH."

Wolverine's feral anger helped him survive an explosion akin to an atomic bomb.

NITRO

But in Wolverine's eyes, this whole mess was the fault of one man—Nitro. After all, he was the Super Villain who had detonated his explosive powers, killing hundreds of Stamford residents. So instead of participating in the deadly war games with his fellow Avengers, or sitting on the sidelines with his fellow X-Men, Wolverine began to track Nitro, following his scent to Big Sur, California.

When Logan attacked him, Nitro immediately unleashed his powers, engulfing Wolverine in a lethal fireball, and reducing his body to little more than a metal skeleton. Using his healing factor, he knit himself back together, and viciously assaulted Nitro, prepared to kill the villain for his sins. But Nitro had information: Someone had supplied him with Mutant Growth Hormone, aka steroids for the super-powered set.

Mutant Growth Hormone (MGH) is a highly illegal drug that grants humans super powers for a short period, and gives superhumans a power-boosting high.

Captain America finally ended the fighting and turned himself in to Iron Man, after seeing the devastation they had caused in New York City.

NAMOR

Before Wolverine could learn the name of Nitro's drug supplier, he was attacked by Namor, the King of Atlantis, and two of his sleeper human agents, Janus and Amir. Knocking Wolverine out, Namor departed for Atlantis with Nitro, determined to punish the villain for the death of his cousin, the New Warrior Namorita. Though Logan followed the sea king with the aid of an Iron Man suit, he later decided that Nitro's fate should be left up to Namor.

WALTER DECLUN

After learning from Namor that successful businessman and head of the Damage Control Super Hero clean-up service, Walter Declun, had given Nitro the MGH, Logan headed to the corrupt CEO's Manhattan office. Learning that Super Hero fights meant big money to Declun, Wolverine killed the scheming businessman, despite Declun trying to even the odds by taking the very drug he peddled.

Gaining an Iron Man suit from Tony Stark, Wolverine used the armor to journey underwater to Atlantis.

167

A warmongering race of aliens with no planet to call their own, the Skrulls have often set their sights on the lush planet Earth. With the uncanny ability to change their shape and appearance to perfectly replicate any human they wish, the Skrulls have proved to be worthy adversaries for Earth's Super Heroes.

Although they could perfectly imitate physical traits and vocal patterns, Skrulls could not mimic the actual powers of their targets. This fact, along with their inability to match the exact scents of those they were impersonating, made their presence easier to detect, especially for individuals with enhanced senses, like Wolverine. However, in time, the Skrulls began to delve into the science of superpowers, experimenting on their own race's mutants, as well as with the DNA of Earth's own heroes.

Wolverine vs. the Skrulls

When Wolverine and the X-Men were frozen in suspended animation while returning to Earth from a battle off-world, a band of Skrulls kidnapped Logan and handed him over to their partner at the time, the mutant overlord Apocalypse. A well-trained Skrull was put in Logan's place as part of a mission to gain information on the X-Men. Having undergone months of psychiatric conditioning, the Skrull had even taken on Logan's mannerisms, making him indistinguishable from the feral mutant.

What a Skrull lacks in physical power, he makes up for with subterfuge and craftiness. However, none is a physical match for Logan by himself.

A Skrull-imposter Wolverine fought side by side with the X-Men for days, only giving his teammates the slightest hint that something was wrong. Able to mimic Logan's bone claws and athletic abilities without the use of superpowers, the Skrull Wolverine's cover was only blown when he was fatally wounded in a battle with the Horseman Death, who was actually the true Wolverine in an altered form.

It was the Skrulls' most ambitious plan to date, a hostile takeover on the grandest scale, and Wolverine was caught right in the middle. When his former partner Elektra was revealed to be a Skrull in disguise, Logan and his fellow New Avengers became rife with suspicion. Discovering more and more of these alien sleeper agents among them, the heroes of Earth were caught completely off guard when the Skrulls launched a systematic attack, targeting the humans' technology as well as their now well-developed sense of paranoia. In the wake of the enemy-breeding Civil War, the heroes would once again have to learn how to trust

Even Wolverine's heightened senses couldn't detect the new breed of

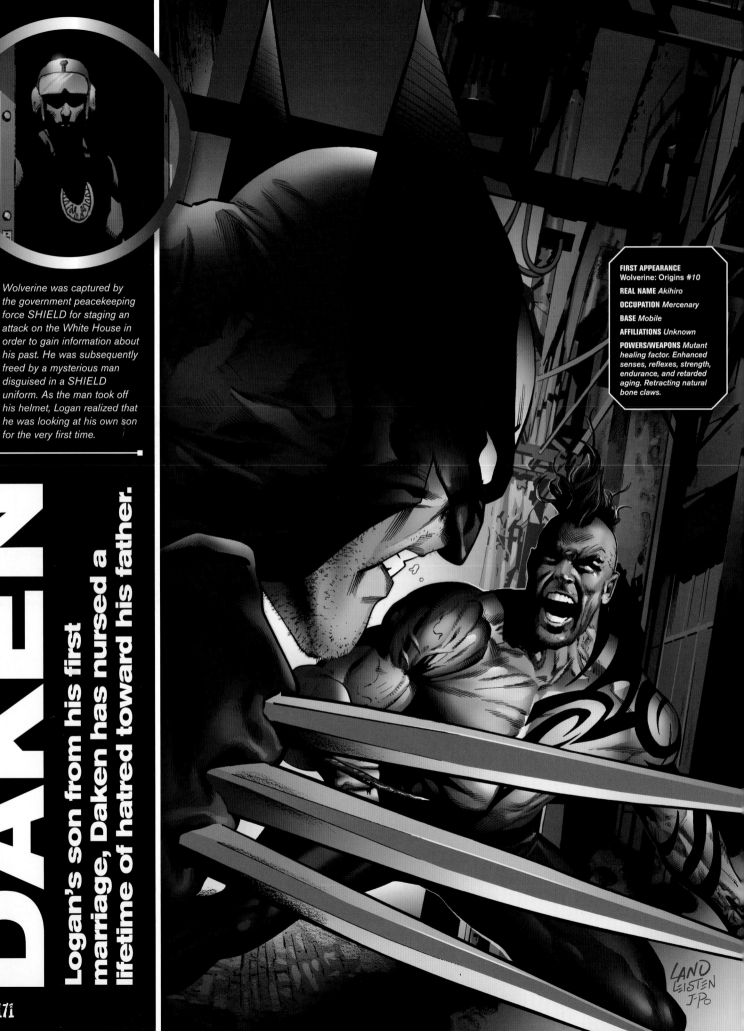

Wolverine was captured by the government peacekeeping force SHIELD for staging an attack on the White House in order to gain information about his past. He was subsequently freed by a mysterious man disguised in a SHIELD uniform. As the man took off his helmet, Logan realized that he was looking at his own son for the very first time.

FIRST APPEARANCE
Wolverine: Origins #10
REAL NAME *Akihiro*
OCCUPATION *Mercenary*
BASE *Mobile*
AFFILIATIONS *Unknown*
POWERS/WEAPONS *Mutant healing factor. Enhanced senses, reflexes, strength, endurance, and retarded aging. Retracting natural bone claws.*

DAKEN

Logan's son from his first marriage, Daken has nursed a lifetime of hatred toward his father.

A natural born killer, Daken appears to possess all of Wolverine's rage, yet none of his conscience.

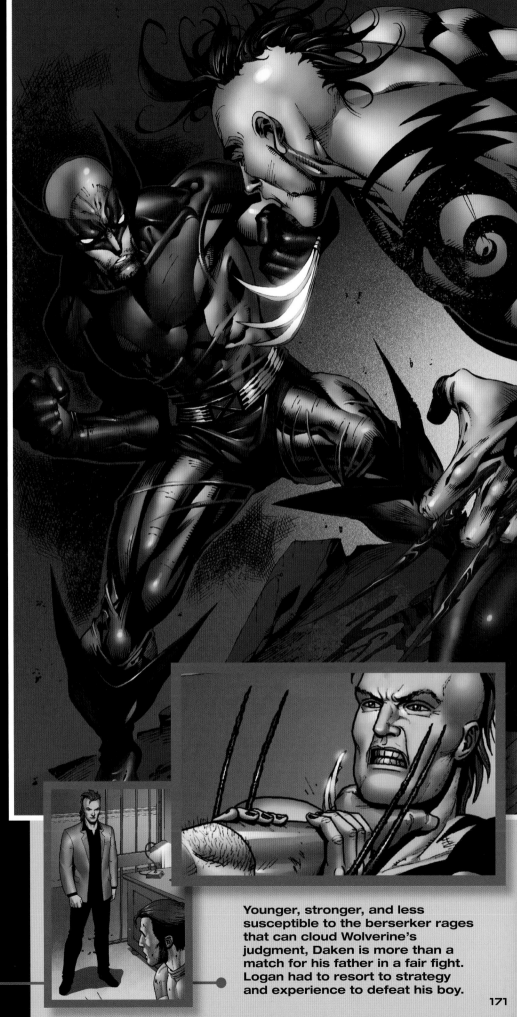

On their first meeting, Daken sliced open Wolverine's stomach, leaving him for dead. On their second, he stabbed him through the chest with his claws. Logan's relationship with his newly discovered son was not going well. Of course, it didn't have much to build on in the first place.

When Wolverine's wife, Itsu, was murdered by the Winter Soldier, who had been hired by the enigmatic master manipulator Romulus, Logan assumed his unborn son was dead. In truth, the boy was saved and delivered to a man named Akihira and his wife, Natsumi, in the village of Sendai, Japan. There he grew up with the stigma of being referred to as a mongrel or *daken* by the villagers. Named Akihiro, the boy grew up tormented by his peers, and could not contain the anger inside himself, even killing one of his bullies in a planned murder. When Akihiro killed Akihira and Natsumi's natural-born second child, the parents expelled him from their house, an action that resulted in both of their deaths. That night Romulus chose to present himself to the young mutant, and it was Romulus that Akihiro, now adopting the name Daken, grew to serve willingly.

After his first encounter with Daken in the SHIELD hideout, Wolverine went looking for the Carbonadium Synthesizer, knowing it would help him bring down his wild son without unduly harming him. After further confrontations with Daken, Wolverine called in an old debt and asked the Winter Soldier to shoot Daken with a carbonadium bullet, rendering the angry young mutant paralyzed and powerless. Logan then brought his son to California, determined to keep the boy out of trouble until he could bring down Romulus, and undo the damage his arch foe had done to Daken throughout the boy's life.

Younger, stronger, and less susceptible to the berserker rages that can cloud Wolverine's judgment, Daken is more than a match for his father in a fair fight. Logan had to resort to strategy and experience to defeat his boy.

CYBER

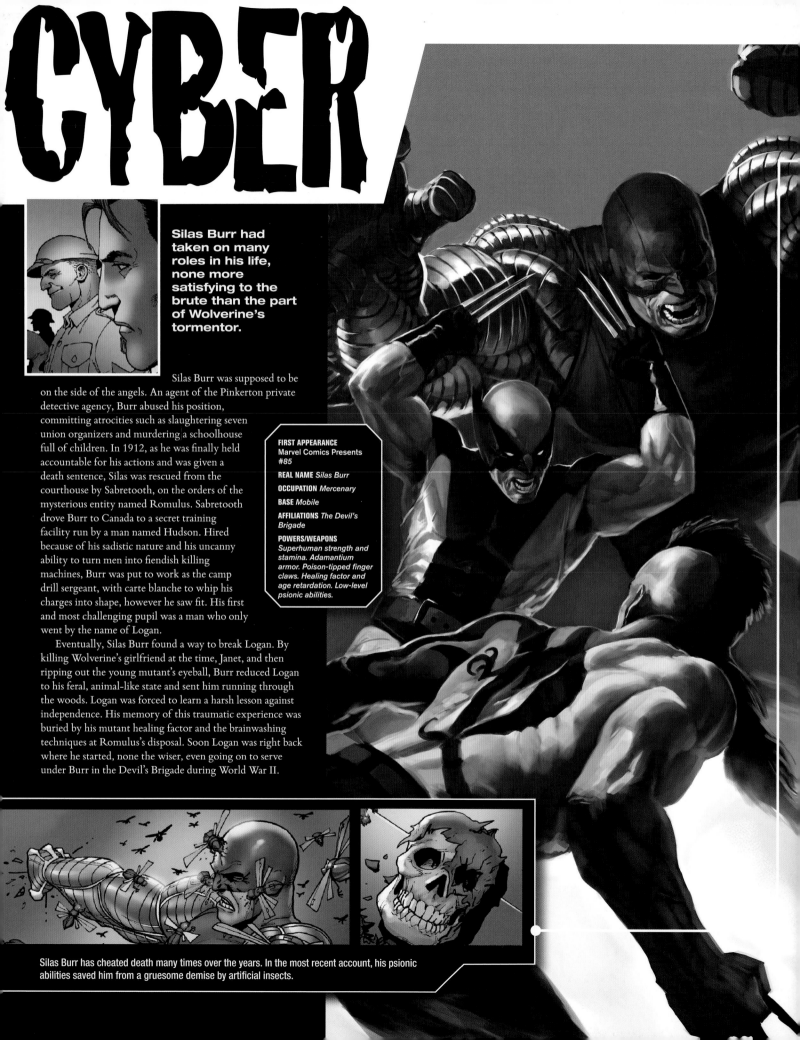

Silas Burr had taken on many roles in his life, none more satisfying to the brute than the part of Wolverine's tormentor.

Silas Burr was supposed to be on the side of the angels. An agent of the Pinkerton private detective agency, Burr abused his position, committing atrocities such as slaughtering seven union organizers and murdering a schoolhouse full of children. In 1912, as he was finally held accountable for his actions and was given a death sentence, Silas was rescued from the courthouse by Sabretooth, on the orders of the mysterious entity named Romulus. Sabretooth drove Burr to Canada to a secret training facility run by a man named Hudson. Hired because of his sadistic nature and his uncanny ability to turn men into fiendish killing machines, Burr was put to work as the camp drill sergeant, with carte blanche to whip his charges into shape, however he saw fit. His first and most challenging pupil was a man who only went by the name of Logan.

Eventually, Silas Burr found a way to break Logan. By killing Wolverine's girlfriend at the time, Janet, and then ripping out the young mutant's eyeball, Burr reduced Logan to his feral, animal-like state and sent him running through the woods. Logan was forced to learn a harsh lesson against independence. His memory of this traumatic experience was buried by his mutant healing factor and the brainwashing techniques at Romulus's disposal. Soon Logan was right back where he started, none the wiser, even going on to serve under Burr in the Devil's Brigade during World War II.

FIRST APPEARANCE
Marvel Comics Presents #85

REAL NAME *Silas Burr*

OCCUPATION *Mercenary*

BASE *Mobile*

AFFILIATIONS *The Devil's Brigade*

POWERS/WEAPONS
Superhuman strength and stamina. Adamantium armor. Poison-tipped finger claws. Healing factor and age retardation. Low-level psionic abilities.

Silas Burr has cheated death many times over the years. In the most recent account, his psionic abilities saved him from a gruesome demise by artificial insects.

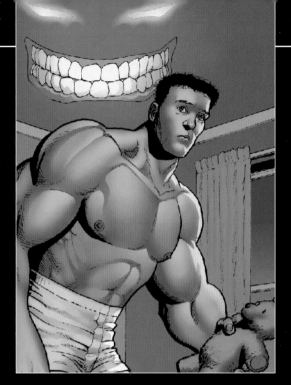

MILO GUNDERSON

Possessing the brain of a child and the body of a superhuman adult, Milo Gunderson was more than his parents could handle. However, when Silas Burr used his psionic abilities to take possession of the boy, Milo became a threat of world proportions. Burr wasted no time in killing Milo's father on the spot.

A perfect specimen save for a bad heart, Milo required medicine to keep him alive. This was a fact Silas Burr was unaware of.

THE TINKERER

After an encounter with Wolverine and Daken, a dying Cyber begged Logan to take him to the Tinkerer, who outfitted Burr with a pacemaker. However, Wolverine had the device made of radioactive carbonadium, to spite his foe.

SUPER VILLAIN

After his assignments from Romulus abruptly ended, Silas Burr started his new life as Cyber.

Possessing a heartless, black soul, and lacking any real feeling for anyone besides himself, Silas Burr found his skills and temperament translated easily to the world of the freelance assassin and mercenary. Armed with the enhanced strength, healing factor, and low-level psionic abilities that he had possessed since childhood, and fitted with a suit of adamantium armor equipped with poison-tipped claws, Burr became Cyber, a Super Villain on a par with the most formidable enemies Wolverine has ever faced.

Some years later, Cyber traveled to Madripoor on a quest to become a powerful player in the drug industry there. As a favor to his friend and crime lord Tyger Tiger, Wolverine decided to spy on a meeting between Cyber and the corrupt General Coy. Wolverine soon recognized the would-be drug supplier as his enemy Silas Burr. During a vicious fight, Cyber cut Wolverine with his finger claws, and simultaneously gave him a free sample of the drug he was peddling. Wolverine staggered into the night, experiencing a twisted nightmare of his past training with Burr. In this hallucinogenic vision, Logan was at a 1950s diner, and was flirting with his girl, a blonde woman named Janet, who rejected him, telling the mutant that she had begun to date their gym teacher, Mr. Cypher.

As Wolverine continued to be haunted by his bizarre dreams, a wild wolf from the forest alerted Tyger Tiger to Wolverine's location, and she helped her friend recover. Returned to full strength, Wolverine once again battled Cyber, plunging the villain into the spilt remains of the drug shipment he was trying to sell to the mob bosses. Cyber retreated into the woods to deal with his drug overdose, a bit more unstable, yet now with enhanced psionic abilities. These came in handy when Cyber was seemingly put to death on the orders of Romulus. He escaped this fate by transferring his consciousness into the mind of boy giant Milo Gunderson.

Primed in his new body, Cyber set out to destroy Romulus, seeking to beat location information out of his former student, Daken.

Wolverine was plagued with dreams about an ancient tribe of dog-like creatures called the Lupine. He determined to go about his business, ridding the world of his mutant adversary Sabretooth, the murderer of Wolverine's long-lost love, Silver Fox. However, the weird dreams refused to go away and Wolverine found it hard to push them to the back of his mind...

ROOOAR?!

As Wolverine and Sabretooth's battle raged across the country, Logan continued to ponder his mysterious dreams. In his visions, each seemingly separated from the other by hundreds of years, a black dog creature would kill a blonde dog creature, all under the watchful eye of some larger canine beast, who seemed to be in overall control.

LUPINE DREAMS

Wolverine's visions of a strange, wolf-like race wouldn't stop. They kept interrupting his life, a violent surge of unconscious memory demanding his attention. And at the center of these dreams remained a single, enigmatic name: Romulus.

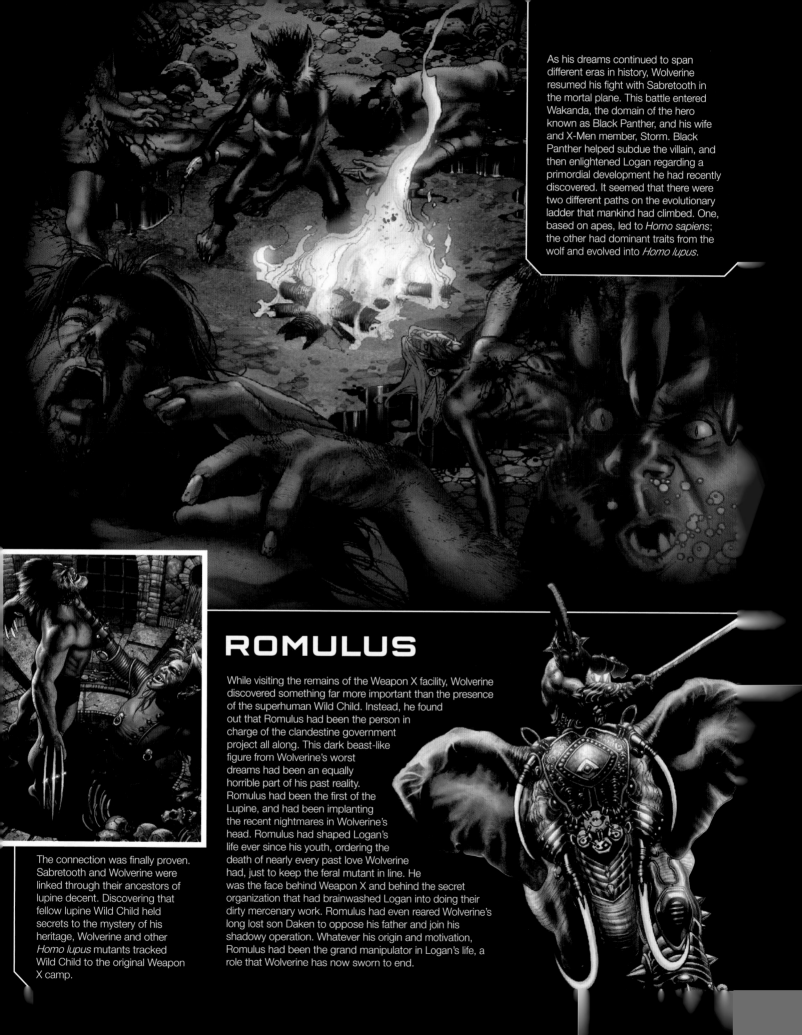

As his dreams continued to span different eras in history, Wolverine resumed his fight with Sabretooth in the mortal plane. This battle entered Wakanda, the domain of the hero known as Black Panther, and his wife and X-Men member, Storm. Black Panther helped subdue the villain, and then enlightened Logan regarding a primordial development he had recently discovered. It seemed that there were two different paths on the evolutionary ladder that mankind had climbed. One, based on apes, led to *Homo sapiens*; the other had dominant traits from the wolf and evolved into *Homo lupus*.

The connection was finally proven. Sabretooth and Wolverine were linked through their ancestors of lupine decent. Discovering that fellow lupine Wild Child held secrets to the mystery of his heritage, Wolverine and other *Homo lupus* mutants tracked Wild Child to the original Weapon X camp.

ROMULUS

While visiting the remains of the Weapon X facility, Wolverine discovered something far more important than the presence of the superhuman Wild Child. Instead, he found out that Romulus had been the person in charge of the clandestine government project all along. This dark beast-like figure from Wolverine's worst dreams had been an equally horrible part of his past reality. Romulus had been the first of the Lupine, and had been implanting the recent nightmares in Wolverine's head. Romulus had shaped Logan's life ever since his youth, ordering the death of nearly every past love Wolverine had, just to keep the feral mutant in line. He was the face behind Weapon X and behind the secret organization that had brainwashed Logan into doing their dirty mercenary work. Romulus had even reared Wolverine's long lost son Daken to oppose his father and join his shadowy operation. Whatever his origin and motivation, Romulus had been the grand manipulator in Logan's life, a role that Wolverine has now sworn to end.

ROARRRR

東奎

As Wolverine followed the trail of fellow lupine mutant Wild Child back to the Weapon X complex, Sabretooth brutally attacked his longtime foe.

DEATH OF SABRETOOTH

Logan had sworn a blood debt against Sabretooth long ago. And finally it was time to collect.

Wolverine and Sabretooth had taken their fight across continents. While discovering the secrets of their lupine ancestry, Logan and his savage companion had traveled from New York to Africa and finally to Canada, where Sabretooth slew Wolverine's friend and fellow X-alumni, Feral. Wolverine could no longer stand idly by while Creed continued to commit atrocity after atrocity. It was time to do something about his lifelong foe, to end their bitter enmity once and for all. And for that, Wolverine would need the Muramasa Blade.

One of the few weapons capable of killing Wolverine, the Muramasa Blade also possessed the ability to nullify Sabretooth's mutant healing factor and thereby carve lasting wounds. After retrieving the sword from Cyclops, Wolverine headed to the one location he knew his enemy could not resist following him to—the Canadian cabin where Sabretooth had killed Logan's former love Silver Fox. Creed took the bait, and he and Logan began a battle unlike any that had gone before. Using the blade, Wolverine severed Sabretooth's arm, and then, as Creed surrendered, decapitated his old foe, uttering one final and appropriate taunt: "Happy birthday."

Wolverine had entrusted the Muramasa Blade to Cyclops.

While at the Department K facility in Canada, Sabretooth made short work of Logan's allies. Wild Child took Alpha Flight alumnus Sasquatch out of commission; Sabretooth bested Thornn and Wolfsbane, killing Feral.

Near the shattered remains of his old Canadian cabin, Wolverine sat and meditated, waiting for his enemy to arrive.

After a fierce battle in which Wolverine demonstrated the Muramasa Blade's power by severing Sabretooth's arm, Creed finally realized his life was over, and showed a rare human emotion as he shed a single tear.

After taking Sabretooth's life, and finally ending their age old war, Wolverine was not satisfied. There was still the matter of Creed's employer, the mysterious Romulus, who was the true reason for all the pain in Logan's long life.

The DEATH of Wolverine

He was a walking dead man, and didn't even know it. As the dust cleared on the Super Hero Civil War, Wolverine's life returned to its usual insanely fast pace. On a favor to his new love, the blue-skinned Atlantean warrior Amir, he traveled to Iraq and encountered the Scimitar (1), a secret terrorist organization that was attempting to rival similar sinister groups such as the Hand, AIM, and Hydra. Discovering that Scimitar was targeting SHIELD director and Super Hero Iron Man, Wolverine boarded a SHIELD helicarrier in order to rescue his old ally, only to discover he had been tricked into boarding a Scimitar air vessel instead. Forced into battle with a masked man clad in adamantium armor, Wolverine watched helplessly as Amir was killed by the warrior's throwing star (2). He blindly charged his opponent, enraged at the all-too-familiar sight of his lovers being butchered. Wolverine then felt something being stuffed into his mouth, but reacted much too late (3). He had just swallowed a bomb, one his attacker did not balk in detonating.

While Logan's physical body lay brain dead, recovered by SHIELD agents, his soul was enjoying a few beers at an empty bar in a purgatory of sorts. There, the astral form of sorcerer supreme Dr. Strange paid the mutant a strange visit, explaining to Wolverine exactly how and why he had been brought to such a place (4). It seemed that back in World War I, Logan had faced a threat on a German field of battle after being dosed with chlorine gas. The threat was a lone man, dressed in a red cloak and armed with nothing more than a broadsword. Logan brazenly charged this new enemy with nothing more than the blades of two bayonets, and actually bested the foe, running the mysterious man through with his own sword. What Logan didn't know at the time was that the man he had killed that day was Lazaer, an anagram for Azrael, the angel of death himself.

Even though he had beaten the angel of death Lazaer once, Wolverine wasn't the type to shy away from a rematch. Since his original duel during World War I, every time Logan suffered a life-threatening injury, his body would mend itself while his soul would travel to purgatory to do battle with Lazaer, and win the chance to save his soul and keep it from passing into the afterlife. However upon his last duel with the angel of death, Wolverine's will had been sapped by the death of his newest love Amir, and Lazaer was finally able to defeat him **(5)**.

After being briefed on his history with Lazaer by Dr. Strange, Wolverine decided to escape his purgatory saloon life and exited out the front door. However he found himself battling different versions of himself **(6)**, from when he first learned he was a mutant, to his time as a guinea pig in the Weapon X program, to when he had been run through by the murderous Hand agent Gorgon. It was during this last encounter that Wolverine realized something about himself had changed. On this occasion, the Hand had used an ancient ritual to bring Wolverine back to life. Present at the ceremony was a woman who had stolen something vital from Logan, something that had made it harder for him to defeat Lazaer each time they fought. Wolverine realized he had to find this woman. At that moment, his soul was reunited with his body in the physical world.

Milking the Hand for information, Wolverine soon learned this female enemy was named Phaedra **(7)**, and that she now worked closely with Scimitar. Following her back to her home, Wolverine attacked Phaedra, only to discover that what she had stolen from him was a piece of his very soul. As Lazaer stepped out of the shadows, revealing he knew Phaedra quite well, Wolverine realized he was outnumbered but not outmatched. Phaedra's frequent resurrections plagued the angel of death's very existence yet, for some reason, Lazaer was unable to kill her. Wolverine did not have the same restrictions and made a deal with the angel of death. He would kill Phaedra **(8)**, and free Lazaer from her meddling if Lazaer would return Logan's soul to him in full. This price Lazaer was glad to pay, making Wolverine a whole man once again. There was only one catch: the next time Wolverine died, it would be for good.

Wolverine did the unthinkable to regain the missing piece of his soul.

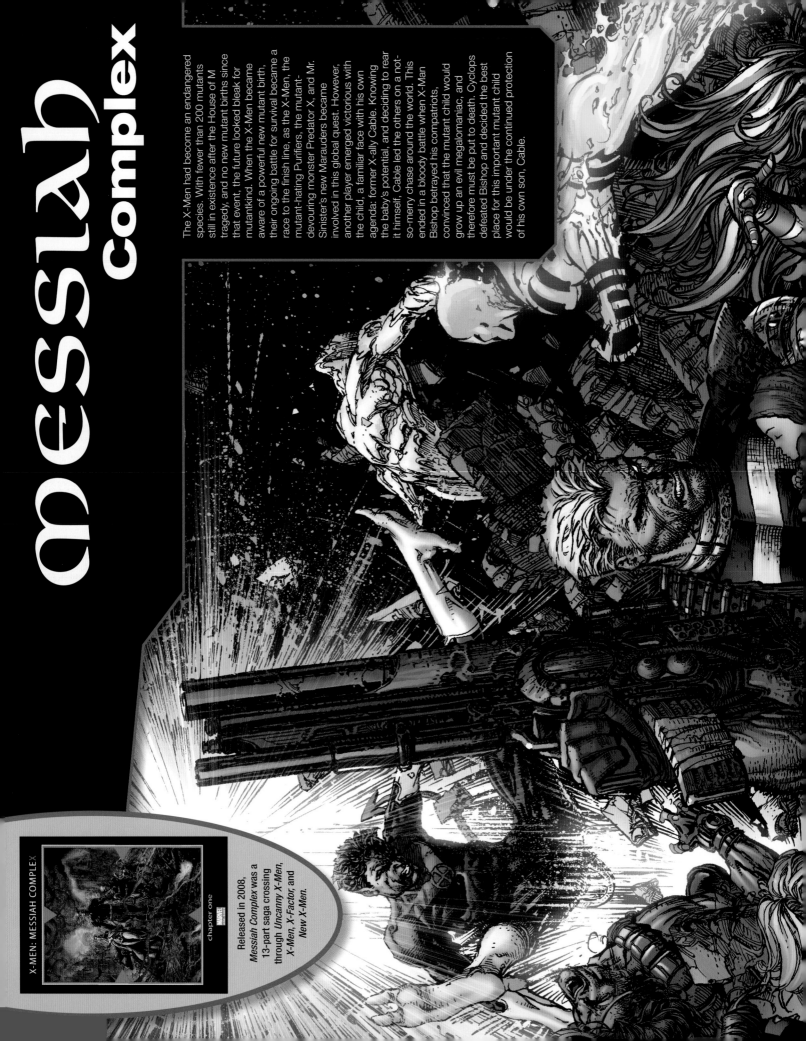

MESSIAH Complex

The X-Men had become an endangered species. With fewer than 200 mutants still in existence after the House of M tragedy, and no new mutant births since that event, the future looked bleak for mutantkind. When the X-Men became aware of a powerful new mutant birth, their ongoing battle for survival became a race to the finish line, as the X-Men, the mutant-hating Purifiers, the mutant-devouring monster Predator X, and Mr. Sinister's new Marauders became involved in this global quest. However, another player emerged victorious with the child, a familiar face with his own agenda: former X-ally Cable. Knowing the baby's potential, and deciding to rear it himself, Cable led the others on a not-so-merry chase around the world. This ended in a bloody battle when X-Man Bishop betrayed his compatriots, convinced that the mutant child would grow up an evil megalomaniac, and therefore must be put to death. Cyclops defeated Bishop and decided the best place for this important mutant child would be under the continued protection of his own son, Cable.

X-MEN: MESSIAH COMPLEX

chapter one

MARVEL

Released in 2008, *Messiah Complex* was a 13-part saga crossing through *Uncanny X-Men, X-Men, X-Factor,* and *New X-Men.*

Never one to be left out of the action, Wolverine was a part of the Messiah Complex from its inception. He fought the Marauders in Alaska at the location of the mutant child's birth and then tracked them to their base in Antarctica. Wolverine went on to fight countless villains for the X-Men's cause, including his old foe Lady Deathstrike and his former teammates Lady Mastermind and Gambit. He also single-handedly defeated the monstrous Predator X, allowing the creature to swallow him in order to attack its vulnerable insides. In the adventure's final moments, Wolverine looked on helplessly as a stray bullet from Bishop's gun pierced the chest of Professor X. Wolverine and his fellow X-Men prayed that their friend and mentor would survive this latest brush with death.

When X-23 first encountered the X-Men, she wore a costume similar to the one Wolverine stole from the alien Fang when he first battled the Imperial Guard of the Shi'ar race.

X·23

She was created by the Weapon X program to be the most dangerous young woman alive. And with Wolverine's DNA, what choice did X-23 have?

ORIGIN

Hired by an offshoot of the Weapon X program, mutant geneticist Dr. Sarah Kinney began working to clone the project's greatest success, Wolverine.

Finding it too difficult to clone a male, Dr. Kinney altered the test subject to be a female. Under pressure from her superiors, she also volunteered to give birth to the mutant child.

Thus X-23 was born, a lab rat to be poked and prodded daily and, from the age of seven, trained in the ways of deadly combat.

Her every action manipulated, X-23's emotions were also tampered with by the Weapon X heads.

By concocting a scent that drove her feral nature into a blind fury, the scientists at Weapon X forced X-23 to kill her own sensei, as a warning against her growing independence.

Raised in captivity as something less than human, X-23 was to be the ultimate weapon, and the ultimate experiment for the Weapon X project.

When her claws first emerged, they knew she would be a success. And soon she was the perfect little assassin, able to get in and out of situations unnoticed, her kills almost surgical in their precision. X-23 was a weapon for hire, rented to society's most vile for millions as a premier killing machine. But the Weapon X heads didn't think it through. Despite the lack of ethics and morals they'd ingrained in their subject since her birth, they forgot that the DNA they'd used to create her was that of a hero: Wolverine. And soon, after the death of her sensei, and her refusal to kill a young boy on a mission, X-23 somehow managed to concoct a sliver of a conscience. This sense of right and wrong continued to develop as Dr. Kinney, X-23's biological mother, found herself taking pity on her young daughter, despite her better judgment. Unable to lie to herself that what she was doing was a boon to science or society, Kinney engineered X-23's escape, a plot that cost her her own life. But even as she died, Dr. Sarah Kinney gave X-23 the greatest gift the sheltered child had received in her entire life. The gift of a name: Laura.

Lost on her own and with no shortage of childhood trauma to influence her decisions, X-23 found herself adrift in the world, becoming a prostitute to make ends meet. Helped through her life on the street by a few other NYX gutterpunks, and then brought to Xavier's Mansion by Wolverine himself, the quiet and reserved Laura became one of the newest students in the school for gifted youngsters. She grew to become a valued and treasured part of the New X-Men, fighting alongside other fresh young heroes, such as the chameleon-like Anole, the brash Hellion, and the healer Elixir. Laura even earned a place of respect among her adult contemporaries as well. In the Messiah Complex adventure, Wolverine allowed her to battle one of his most dangerous enemies, the cutthroat Lady Deathstrike. Although X-23 still hasn't quite found her place in the world, her time with the X-Men has given her something she lacked all through her childhood: A family.

FIRST APPEARANCE
X-Men Evolution #40; NYX #3

REAL NAME *Laura Kinney*

OCCUPATION *Adventurer, assassin, prostitute*

BASE *Angel's Aerie in the Colorado Rocky Mountains*

AFFILIATIONS *X-Force, X-Men, The Facility, Weapon X*

POWERS/WEAPONS
Retractable adamantium claws. Accelerated healing ability. Superhuman strength and reflexes.

X-23's claws have been coated in adamantium like Wolverine's claws. However, unlike him, X-23 only has two claws on each hand.

X-23 possesses an accelerated healing factor, which can mend nearly any injury. Even though the rest of her bones are not all bonded with adamantium like Wolverine's, X-23 is still a near-indestructible killing machine, trained in the martial arts since age seven.

X-23's possesses superhuman strength and stamina. In addition to her hand claws, she can extend a claw from the top of each foot. Each blade is laced with adamantium.

18

Despite protests from Wolverine, the man who shares her DNA, X-23 now serves on the covert action team, X-Force. There her deadly talents are often put to good use.

Mystique

A chameleon by nature, Mystique's features are as elusive as her motives.

She's been on just about every side there is. Born centuries ago, Raven Darkholme, the adaptive mutant who would become known as Mystique, has lived a life of ever-changing principles. When she and Logan first met, it was as targets of a firing squad in Mexico in 1921. Logan had been sentenced to death for stealing a horse, while Mystique's only crime was her mutant appearance. She was able to slip out of her restraints, and Logan made quick work of the death squad, his healing factor taking care of the fresh gun wounds. Afterwards, Logan and Mystique became acquainted over dinner, and soon traveled to Kansas City, where they set up shop with a band of misfit grifters that Raven knew well. It was in that Wild West town that Mystique and Logan first began their romance.

Normally finding themselves on opposite ends of the law, Wolverine and Mystique nonetheless have an undeniable chemistry, one that has gotten them both into trouble.

WANTED!

(Dead or Alive)

$1,000,000 REWARD

BANKING ON IT

With Logan signed up with her merry men of con artists, Mystique soon had her eyes on the big prize—the Federal Reserve Bank. Reluctantly going along with his lover's scheme, Logan helped the manipulative mutant and her grifters storm the bank. However, the cops were waiting for them. Logan had set Mystique up, realizing that his lover had been playing him for a sucker since the day she had orchestrated their first meeting. Despite the heavy police presence, the elusive, evasive Mystique still managed to slip away into the night.

FIRST APPEARANCE
Ms. Marvel #16

REAL NAME Unrevealed; her most frequent alias is Raven Darkholme

OCCUPATION Mercenary

BASE Mobile

POWERS/WEAPONS Mutant shape-changing and age retardation abilities. Immune to drugs and poison. Rapid healing abilities. Expert martial artist. Excellent weapon and acting skills.

"Jus' shake some grenadine into a white wine for the lady."

Get Mystique!

Wolverine's patience with Mystique finally ran out after Raven had spent some time with the X-Men, leading them to believe that she had reformed. Instead, after earning their trust, Mystique shot her own adopted daughter, Rogue, during an attack by her new team of deadly Marauders. In order to make Raven pay for her crimes, Wolverine began a hunt for Mystique that led him all the way to the deserts of the Middle East.

"...I'm sure you'll figure out what the pistol's for."

"I'll see you in HELL, Logan."

After a fierce battle involving enough spent ammunition to wipe out a platoon, Wolverine finally gained the upper hand on Mystique. Left bleeding and wounded in the desert, Mystique had only one option–to take her own life with a handgun Wolverine had left her.

PART-TIME LOVERS

Mystique and Wolverine have usually met on the field of battle as a part of their respective teams, the X-Men and the Brotherhood of Evil Mutants. But from time to time, Wolverine and Mystique have taken a night or two off to rekindle their nearly century-old attraction. On one occasion, when Logan was spending a few hours off-duty from the X-Men at one of his favorite dive bars, the Auger Inn, Mystique interrupted his game of pool, disguised as an attractive stranger. Knowing her scent despite her appearance, Logan played along, and the two spent a romantic night together in a nearby hotel. Mystique amused herself by adopting the appearance of two of Wolverine's other loves, Jean Grey and Silver Fox, before she decided to reveal the real motive behind her visit: she needed Wolverine's help in an extra-dimensional battle against the bizarre villain Mojo.

CHAPTER **SIX**

Wolverine in the Future

Alternate Futures

Wolverine has unlocked many secrets of his past. Yet his future remains a blank slate, changing with each decision he makes in the present.

Days of Future Past
Logan got his first glimpse into a possible future when an adult Kitty Pryde traveled back in time to possess a younger version of herself. This Kitty hailed from a dystopian future overrun with mutant-killing Sentinels. In this future, Kitty was married to Colossus and teamed with an aged version of Wolverine, Magneto, and a familiar looking redhead named Rachel Summers. She ultimately journeyed back to the past to prevent the assassination of the mutant-hating senator Robert Kelly by Mystique and her newly reformed Brotherhood of Evil Mutants.

Old Man Logan
In another futuristic landscape, Wolverine became a pacifist after a horrible battle that claimed the lives of many of his friends. Living on a farm and paying rent to the corrupt Hulk Gang, Logan was roped into an adventure alongside former Avengers ally Hawkeye.

Wolverine's Future Death
As Kitty Pryde continued her adventures in the days of future past, the X-Men realized the scope of the world this future survivor hailed from. It was a world in which all the heroes had been wiped out. It was a world in which an anti-mutant fervor had taken hold of the populace, instigating a resurgence in the use of Sentinels, until none but Rachel Summers remained. Even Wolverine met his end at the fiery hands of these robotic murderers.

Wolverine: The End

Wolverine was getting old. If his aging body wasn't proof enough for the feral mutant, then attending the funeral of longtime enemy Victor Creed certainly was. After being handed an envelope by Sabretooth's lawyer, Logan followed a trail back to his own dilapidated boyhood home in Alberta, Canada. From there, a trail of clues led him to a mountain in Japan where he encountered a powerful mutant that went by the name of the White Ghost. After Wolverine was thoroughly beaten by his opponent, the Ghost revealed that he was Wolverine's supposedly long-deceased brother, John Howlett.

Wolverine's years caught up to him during the future reality of "The End." He found he was no longer the hunter of his youth. Now he was scarcely able to catch anything without a trap, and hardly able to deal with the pain of retracting his now broken and worn claws.

Logan rejected his brother's request to join him, realizing that his long-lost sibling was a megalomaniac bent on destroying part of Nevada to gain dominance over the stock market. Instead, Wolverine ran his brother through with his claws, killing any chance for a happy ending.

ULTIMATE
WOLVERINE

It was the Ultimate experiment. In an alternate reality, Wolverine was given a clean slate. But no matter what realm he was born in, Logan would always remain a tortured soul.

The Ultimate Universe was created in order to revitalize the heroes of the Marvel Universe by starting them over, and removing decades worth of continuity and backstory that could possibly bog the characters down. In this newly minted world, Wolverine still found his way to the X-Men, although initially joining as an assassin for Magneto, before seeing the error of his ways.

In August of 1943, as the Allied forces invaded Sicily, James Howlett was among their number. He was caught looting a nearby building and arrested. Taken to Canada and entered into their Weapon X program, Howlett was experimented on, and his genes were mutated, granting him his healing factor. In effect, James Howlett became Mutant Zero, the first mutant of the Ultimate Universe.

Discovered by the X-Men when they helped him avoid recapture at the hands of Weapon X, Wolverine soon joined their ranks. Becoming a staunch believer in Xavier's plan to create a peaceful mutant/human co-existence, Logan rejected Magneto's assignment to murder Professor X and converted to the side of the angels. And he soon got the chance to prove his new loyalties when Magneto attacked Washington DC and turned the human's mutant-hunting Sentinel robots against them. Together, the X-Men defeated Magneto's forces while Professor X himself killed his former friend.

Originally attracted to Logan's bad boy image, Jean Grey wasted no time before embarking on a romance with Wolverine. This relationship didn't sit too well with Jean's would-be suitor, Cyclops. He quit the X-Men after an argument with Professor Xavier, believing he wasn't wanted on the team any longer. Eventually Cyclops returned to his friends, but he and Logan would only ever become uneasy allies at best.

However, Magneto wasn't dead. A true pacifist at heart, Charles Xavier had simply reprogrammed his old friend's mind and made him into a gentle soul. But when the Brotherhood of Mutants rediscovered their former leader, they were able to unblock Magneto's mind, and return his original personality. As Magneto renewed his war on humanity, the X-Men found themselves on the run from the law, hunted by the government's super-soldiers, the Ultimates.

When first they met, it was in Times Square, in a ferocious battle versus Sabretooth. When next they met, it was in a mall food court. Despite coming from two very different corners of the world, Ultimate Spider-Man and Wolverine teamed up many times over the years, and as their pairings became significantly weirder, the two began to respect each other as allies. During one memorable partnership, Wolverine and Spider-Man switched bodies after Logan angered Jean Grey: Jean put Logan's mind in the place he least wanted it to be, and Peter Parker's body was the temporary unlucky recipient.

AFTERWORD

When I first met him, Wolverine really didn't make a good first impression. Actually, if I'm to be perfectly honest, the little guy scared the pants off me. I remember the issue clearly, if not fondly: *Marvel Comics Presents* #10. Investing my entire week's allowance on its bright purple cover, I quickly cracked the comic open, only to be greeted with a horrific image from the issue's Man-Thing tale depicting a man with dozens of bone-like roots protruding sharply out of his skin. The scene shocked my sensitive fourth grade constitution, and just like that, I was done with Wolverine for years, finding the mutant guilty by association.

Today Logan is easily one of my favorite characters in all comics, but I still maintain that the feral mutant doesn't always give the best first impression. At first glance, Wolverine seems like just another slash 'em up anti-hero with an attitude, but when he's handled by writers who understand him, Logan becomes one of the most three-dimensional personalities in the medium, a creature of contradiction proving, like Whitman, that he too contains multitudes.

It's that portrait of Wolverine that I tried to paint with this book. To put his complex history in plain sight, both the good and the bad, and hopefully clear up a few people's misconceptions in the process.

And as my argument draws to its close, I'd be remiss if I didn't mention a few of the people who made it possible. I'd like to thank the editorial and design staff across the pond at DK, for their flexibility in working around my wedding schedule; Mark Beazley at Marvel for lending me a portion of his personal collection; and my beautiful and patient wife, Dorothy, who didn't even think to complain when I brought along a duffle bag full of Wolverine comics to read on the beach on our honeymoon. And thanks also to you, the reader. I hope you enjoyed getting to know Logan, and that this experience was a positive one for you. But if not, that's the beauty of comics. There's always next month for a new first impression.

Matthew K. Manning

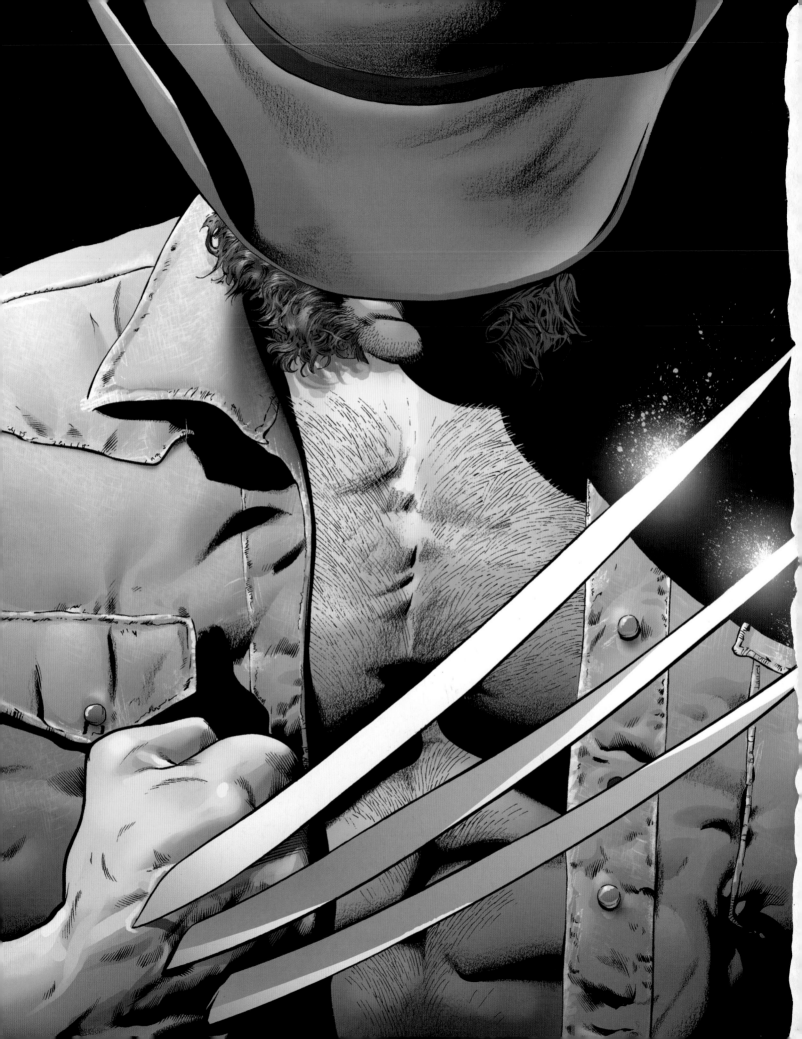